REASONING WITH GOD

REASONING WITH GOD

A special invitation from God for understanding
the Bible, overcoming doubt, and
answering skeptics

Bill Cohen

Table of Contents

Introduction

God says He wants us to "reason" with Him, *Is 1:18*, *"Come now, and let us reason together, saith the Lord: though your sins be as scarlet, they shall be as white as snow; though they be red like crimson, they shall be as wool."* But what does "reasoning" really mean, and why is it so important?

Merriam-Webster defines reasoning as: "The process of thinking about something in a logical way to form a conclusion or judgment; the ability of the mind to think and understand things in a logical way."

God has given us the Bible to reason with, *1 Thes 5:21*, *"Prove all things; hold fast that which is good"* and for the times we are confused, He has sent us the Holy Spirit to guide us through His Word, *Jn 16:13*, *"Howbeit when he, the Spirit of truth, is come, he will guide you into all truth: for he shall not speak of himself; but whatsoever he shall hear, that shall he speak: and he will shew you things to come."* God has given us these two witnesses, so that our faith has a solid foundation, which will be able to withstand the floods of doubt and the winds of dispute brought by the skeptics of this world.

In other words, we are not being disobedient or ungodly when our instincts tell us to reason with the Bible because we feel some conflict between what we think the Bible says and what we believe. Our reasoning does not change the meaning of the Bible, only our understanding of it. It is an important element in overcoming our doubt and it is the key to answering skeptics. How can we possibly minister to someone or share the gospel without reasoning with him or her? Simply reciting scripture is not effective. Remember, God created us to think and question. Doing so is not a spiritual shortcoming, if we are humble and respectful in the process; it is our spiritual calling.

We can look to a good relationship between a child and a parent to better understand this concept. The ideal relationship should be one where the child obeys the parent and questions anything they do not understand. There comes a time when the child is ready to begin asking why the parent is directing them to do or not do something because that child is ready to hear and reason with the answer. This gives the parent a teaching moment, a chance to discuss the repercussions of the actions the child is about to take or avoid. This is how we learn to have the judgment necessary to keep us away from evil and harm. Of course, when the child is young, there are more "whys" than the parent would like, however, in time, the child learns to limit the "whys" to the more important unanswered questions. When children ask the same question many times, it is because they still have doubts about the answers they have been given. This questioning is an important element in the process of becoming the people they were created capable of becoming. It is no different in our relationship with God and His Word; we are children learning to understand when to ask questions as we learn to better understand our Father's Word.

Following blindly is not godly; it is the opposite of what God is asking us to do. Saying "the right things" and going with the flow might look good on the surface and fool some people, but it is like a house built on sand, *Matt 7:24-27, "Therefore whosoever heareth these sayings of mine, and doeth them, I will liken him unto a wise man, which built his house upon a rock: And the rain descended, and the floods came, and the winds blew, and beat upon that house; and it fell not: for it was founded upon a rock. And every one that heareth these sayings of mine, and doeth them not, shall be likened unto a foolish man, which built his house upon the sand: And the rain descended, and the floods came, and the winds blew, and beat upon that house; and it fell: and great was the fall of it."*

As churchgoers and believers, we often avoid critical thinking, questioning, and reasoning. We are afraid of seeming foolish or uninformed, it is easier go along and it helps us avoid difficult discussions and conflicts. But, that does not make it right. We simply cannot be complete Christians without reasoning. So, we need to come together to discuss our ideas with open minds and a willingness to listen, instead of just wanting to change everyone else's minds. True reasoning only occurs when we allow our minds to receive and process new information and perspectives. When that happens, everyone involved gets closer to the Truth.

God does not want us to just memorize the Bible without thinking and He surely does not want us to accept anyone's biblical propaganda. He calls us to reason. God wants us to think about what He is telling us, so that we might come to the Truth that He is love and He loves us. Reasoning is a lifetime journey of becoming the person He created us capable of becoming.

The message of the Bible, or God's "love letter" to us, is God loves us and desires our love, *1 Jn 4:7-8, "Beloved, let us love one another: for love is of God; and every one that loveth is born of God, and knoweth God. He that loveth not knoweth not God; for God is love."* Reasoning with His Word allows us to discover who He is and the depth of His love for us. We then come to the realization that an awesome God, capable of doing all things, has created us to become members of His eternal family. This is how we learn to love Him, *1 Jn 4:19, "We love him, because he first loved us"*; to love ourselves and our neighbors, *Matt 19:19b, "Thou shalt love thy neighbour as thyself"*; and eventually to love our enemies, *Lk 6:27, "But I say unto you which hear, Love your enemies, do good to them which hate you"*. We begin to understand this life and all the disparate things we see happening in this world.

Reasoning with God makes our path clearer, as we move nearer to our true selves. The challenge we face on this journey is to understand that it is not about us, it is about God creating His eternal family. When we finally understand we are part of something bigger, we are better able to understand the message of the cross and can begin to take our reasoning to others. Our current thinking is not perfect, neither is theirs, however, together we all get closer to perfection.

God created us, He knows the answers to all of our questions and He gave us His Word to reason with, in honesty without ulterior motives, so that we might find the Truth, 2 Cor 1:12, *"For our rejoicing is this, the testimony of our conscience, that in simplicity and godly sincerity, not with fleshly wisdom, but by the grace of God, we have had our conversation in the world, and more abundantly to you-ward."*

The purpose of this book is to encourage each of us to honestly reason with God and each other, not just for our own benefit, but, also, to promote a more perfect common understanding of God's way for all of His church. Ultimately, there can be no conflicts in our understanding of God's Word, for there are no conflicts in God's Word. We are one body in Christ, 1 Cor 12:25, 31, *"That there should be no schism in the body; but that the members should have the same care one for another...But covet earnestly the best gifts: and yet shew I unto you a more excellent way."* Not many different excellent ways, one more excellent way.

The message of the cross is unity, calling all who have chosen faith over fear to put on the whole armor of God, *Eph 6:11, "Put on the whole armour of God, that ye may be able to stand against the wiles of the devil."* Lest we be guilty of scattering, *Matt 12:30, "He that is not with me is against me; and he that gathereth not with me scattereth abroad."*

The process of surrendering to His Truth has led me to write this book and has allowed me to experience what I believe the writers of the Bible did when they first sat down to record God's words. I know this sounds a bit arrogant, however, please let me explain.

When I first felt the calling to write this book, a great weight of responsibility came upon me. I began to understand what Job meant in, *Job 13:3, "Surely I would speak to the Almighty, and I desire to reason with God."* Doing what God asks us to do is not always easy, but it is always very important. So, the idea that I could refuse was not one I could entertain.

As the words began to pour out of me, they were confused and overwhelmed with traces of me. I was trying to take God's words and somehow make them better. When the first draft was done I felt some relief. Then, I read it and was dismayed at the amount of me that was in it. The great weight of responsibility was back. Over and over I reread, rewrote and removed any part of me I could find in each draft. Each iteration of the book was better, however, it did not properly represent what I was being called to write, somehow I needed to figure out how to get the "fleshly wisdom" out, *2 Cor 1:12, "For our rejoicing is this, the testimony of our conscience, that in simplicity and godly sincerity, not with fleshly wisdom, but by the grace of God, we have had our conversation in the world, and more abundantly to you-ward."* All scripture quoted in this book comes from the King James Version of the Bible.

I am sure the Biblical writers felt this same pressure. I now pray for you to consider this completed work with God foremost in your mind, focusing on His words, not mine.

Articles are referenced for further study on topics mentioned throughout the book. The actual URL's can be found in Appendix A of this book.

Does God Really Exist?

Before we can truly begin reasoning with God, we must first believe He exists, *Heb 11:6*, *"But without faith it is impossible to please him: for he that cometh to God must believe that he is, and that he is a rewarder of them that diligently seek him."* So, we begin by first deciding on the question of His existence, which will lead us to either belief or denial. Without this first step, we are only reading to find the errors, rather than reading to find the Truth.

He told us, *Gen 1:1*, *"In the beginning God created the heaven and the earth."* Can we reason with what He told us He created to find the proof?

We can look to the heavens to see the beauty and the wonder of our universe, there is a URL in Appendix A for further study labeled: Hubblesite Of Images.[1] The links being provided in Appendix A of this book are meant to allow for further study and should not be taken with blind faith, and neither should the work being presented here. If God created the stars and the planets, they would be predictable. When we look to our skies, do we see a complicated, beautiful, and organized system, or random chance and chaos that has led to disorder and decay? The beautiful creation we see has predictable outcomes, which are meant to help us believe He exists. Only a creator could have brought the stars and planets to this point, *Deut 3:24*, *"O Lord God, thou hast begun to shew thy servant thy greatness, and thy mighty hand: for what God is there in heaven or in earth, that can do according to thy works, and according to thy might?"* God did this so we might discover Him in His creation and because His love for us demands it. From the time of Socrates' idea of a first mover until now, the only logical and probable answer to how things came into being, and are so perfectly arranged, is a creator; a first mover. It takes a huge leap of faith to believe that everything in our skies evolved to this point, after billions of years of random chaos, as a result of some "out of nothing" big bang. Can anything appear, without a first mover, out of nothing?

The world we live in today is best explained from a mathematical perspective, Job 38:5, 18, *"Who hath laid the measures thereof, if thou knowest? or who hath stretched the line upon it? Hast thou perceived the breadth of the earth? declare if thou knowest it all."* Everything in this world fits together in such a precise way only a creator in love with mathematics could have created it.

As an example, the balance that sustains life on this planet, in a self-correcting way, is nothing short of a miracle. The air we breathe is composed of molecules of different gases, the most common being nitrogen (78%), oxygen (about 21%), argon (almost 1%), and carbon dioxide (just less than .5%) in the perfect balance to sustain life as we know it. We need this exact balance of gases. When we exhale carbon dioxide the plants take it in to use in the photosynthesis process, and in return, they give off the oxygen we need as waste, *Rom 1:20, "For the invisible things of him from the creation of the world are clearly seen, being understood by the things that are made, even his eternal power and Godhead; so that they are without excuse:"* Paul is telling us we can look at all of the invisible things that exist in our world to prove God's existence. Our attempts to verify His existence will be rewarded and those unwilling to make the attempt will be without excuse.

"The person who is a consistent evolutionist will attribute the many wonders of our planet (the earth's surface temperature, tilt and rotation, atmosphere, ocean, and crust) to the unguided chance. This conclusion, though not impossible, takes a great deal of faith in extremely improbable events. It is akin to supposing that the Mona Lisa came into existence from globs of paint hurled at a canvas. The creationist, on the other hand, will recognize that the only rational deduction from the data is that the marvels of the earth owe their origin to the intelligence and handiwork of God. It was the psalmist who said: *"In His hand are the deep places of the earth; the strength of the hills is His also. The sea is His, and He made it, and His hands formed the dry land. Oh, come, let us worship and bow down; let us kneel before the Lord our maker"* Psalm 95:4-6." For the complete discussion, check out the whole article written by Stuart E. Nevins, who holds both B.S. and M.S. degrees in geology, and at this writing is the Assistant Professor of Geology at Christian Heritage College: <u>Planet Earth Plan or Accident?</u>[2]

Gen 1:27, "So God created man in his own image, in the image of God created he him; male and female created he them." Our human bodies are another miracle that requires the atheist to have a lot of faith to believe we came into being from a random series of accidents. Our ability to see is nothing short of impossible. Only a creative being could design and construct this one small part of our bodies. Now, expand that to the whole body and the fact that it fits together so perfectly. How does an atheist explain the intervening iterations of the evolving beings they believe in? How were those beings able to get enough food to survive until their eyes evolved? Where is the evidence of these intervening iterations in our world today? The same thought process could be applied to the intervening iterations of the digestive system, etc. To learn about the detailed workings of the eye: How the Eye Works.[3]

Gen 6:3, "Then the LORD said, My Spirit will not contend with man forever, for he is mortal; his days will be a hundred and twenty years." This verse explains the Hayflick Phenomenon as described in Wikipedia: *"The Hayflick limit was discovered by Leonard Hayflick in 1961, at the Wistar Institute, Philadelphia, when Hayflick demonstrated that a population of normal human fetal cells in a cell culture divide between 40 and 60 times. It then enters a senescence phase. Each mitosis shortens the telomeres on the DNA of the cell. Telomere shortening in humans eventually makes cell division impossible, and it is presumed to correlate with aging."* It is interesting how Professor Hayflick's discovery led him to use human DNA to estimate our maximum life expectancy to be about 120 years and that is exactly what God told us some 3,500 years ago, after the flood. Only one person in modern history, Jeanne Calment, is documented to have lived past 120 years, from 1875 to 1997, 122 years.

The average American Seventh Day Adventist lives 10 years longer than the average American. Link to the Huffington Post article: <u>What the Adventists Get Right.</u>[4] Coincidence, or are they choosing to accept God's offer for a longer, healthier life? *Prov 3:1-2, "My son, forget not my law; but let thine heart keep my commandments: For length of days, and long life, and peace, shall they add to thee."* The Adventists decision to follow God's way produces verifiable evidence of God's existence. Those not accepting this as part of the proof of God's existence are ignoring a very valuable piece of evidence. There are more than a million Seventh Day Adventists in the US. This is too large of a sampling to ignore. Oh, by the way, this denomination is the fastest growing Church in the USA: <u>Fastest Growing Church In US.</u>[5]

Is 45:19, "I have not spoken in secret, in a dark place of the earth; I did not say to the seed of Jacob, Seek Me in vain; I, the Lord, speak righteousness, I declare things that are right." God gave us His Word, so that we might find Him in it. He is not hiding His Truth from us; almost everyone in this world has access to it, if they would only seek Him, *Rev 3:20, "Behold, I stand at the door, and knock: if any man hear my voice, and open the door, I will come in to him, and will sup with him, and he with me."* My experience has been in total agreement with Isaiah, in that, I have never met anyone who has read the Bible with the honest desire to understand God and then told me they do not believe in the existence of God. The question we should be asking is: "Why have atheists refused to read the Bible?"

When we look at a leaf, an eye, a mousetrap, a frog, or a computer, can we really believe any of them were created by the accident of random chaos? We all know a computer cannot evolve into existence, so why do we believe an eye or a frog or other parts of God's creation just evolved into what they are? Remember, we are created in His image, thus we create as evidence of our Creator's existence, we create mousetraps and computers, etc. So, does it not follow that God created us?

Do we not now have dominion over all God told us we would? *Gen 1:26, "And God said, Let us make man in our image, after our likeness: and let them have dominion over the fish of the sea, and over the fowl of the air, and over the cattle, and over all the earth, and over every creeping thing that creepeth upon the earth."* Our arrogance allows us to think we know better than God, but Peter and John are warning us not to think we know better, *Acts 4:19, "But Peter and John answered and said unto them, Whether it be right in the sight of God to hearken unto you more than unto God, judge ye."* I believe God knows best and my life is proof He does, because once I accepted Him as my savior my life starting changing and continues to change for the better.

Micah 6:3, "O My people, what have I done unto thee? And wherein have I wearied thee? Testify against me." and *Jer 2:5, "Thus saith the Lord, What iniquity have your fathers found in me, that they are gone far from me, and have walked after vanity, and are become vain?"* God asks Israel to tell Him what He has done that caused Israel to turn away from Him. What can we say to God when He asks us this question?

He has asked us to love our enemy. He has asked us to care for those less fortunate. He has asked us to treat everyone with respect and to be selfless, not selfish. Where will we go to find anyone who can honestly testify against Him?

Many religious leaders, past and present, have misunderstood and misrepresented God, *Mk 2:16, "And when the scribes and Pharisees saw him eat with publicans and sinners, they said unto his disciples, How is it that he eateth and drinketh with publicans and sinners?"* Jesus came to demonstrate His love and to explain that His Word should not be misrepresented. Jesus treated everyone with respect and love. Some understand His love and accept His invitation. Some do not, *Ps 14:2, "The Lord looked down from heaven upon the children of men, to see if there were any that did understand, and seek God."*

We cannot let those who misunderstand God, whether they are religious leaders or famed atheists, steal the reward God has planned for us. For He does exist and has promised to return: *Rev 22:11-13, "He that is unjust, let him be unjust still: and he which is filthy, let him be filthy still: and he that is righteous, let him be righteous still: and he that is holy, let him be holy still. And, behold, I come quickly; and my reward is with me, to give every man according as his work shall be. I am Alpha and Omega, the beginning and the end, the first and the last."* By telling us "I am" God is telling us He exists.

We could look at the Bible prophecies fulfilled for further evidence of His existence, *Is 14:24, "The Lord of hosts hath sworn, saying, Surely as I have thought, so shall it come to pass; and as I have purposed, so shall it stand:"* and *Mk 13:23, "But take ye heed: behold, I have foretold you all things."* and *Deut 18:18, "I will raise them up a Prophet from among their brethren, like unto thee, and will put my words in his mouth; and he shall speak unto them all that I shall command him."* All prophets were created by God to speak His Word to us, so we might know He exists. But, too many of us have ignored His prophecies, which is leading us on a race to remove God from our everyday lives. Look around this world; are we adding or removing God from our everyday lives?

Not all who claim to be prophets are prophets, *Deut 18:22, "When a prophet speaketh in the name of the Lord, if the thing follow not, nor come to pass, that is the thing which the Lord hath not spoken, but the prophet hath spoken it presumptuously: thou shalt not be afraid of him."* Seeing the future, God warns us about the false prophets who will come to distort His Truth. He tells us how we can know whether He sent a prophet, so we will not be fooled.

Jesus' life is prophecy fulfilled, *Matt 5:17, "Think not that I am come to destroy the law, or the prophets: I am not come to destroy, but to fulfil."* Born of a virgin (*Is 7:14 & Matt 2:1-6*), in Bethlehem (*Micah 5:2 & Matt 2:1-6*), descended from David (*Jer 33:15 & Matt 1:1*), sent by God (*Is 42:13 & Matt 17:5*), sent as our Savior (*Is 43:7, 11 & Lk 2:11*), entered Jerusalem riding on a donkey (*Zech 9:9 & Matt 21:6-9*), rejected by the people (*Ps 118:22 & Matt 21:42*), nailed on a cross (*Ps 22:16 & Jn 20:27*), resurrected (*Ps 16:9-11 & Acts 13:29-31*), and He will return to claim His people (*Matt 24:30*). God asks us all to reason for ourselves. He asks us to challenge everything, including what we see in our world today. For more of the prophecies fulfilled by Jesus: Jesus' Fulfilling Of Bible Prophecy.[6] A quote from this link: "Mathematicians put it this way: 1 person fulfilling 8 prophecies: 1 in 100,000,000,000,000,000: 1 person fulfilling 48 prophecies: 1 chance in 10 to the 157th power, and 1 person fulfilling 300+ prophecies: Only Jesus!"

No one has a monopoly on God's Word; it is only when we honestly reason with God and others that His Word comes to life. So, we need to read His Word, pray about it, and gather with others to discuss it. Then, we will discern the Truth, with the help of the Holy Spirit.

Skeptics claim the Old Testament has been altered to fit with the current understanding of history. However, God has told us, *Matt 5:18, "For verily I say unto you, Till heaven and earth pass, one jot or one tittle shall in no wise pass from the law, till all be fulfilled."* In 1947 a Bedouin boy accidently discovered the Dead Sea Scrolls. It has taken decades for archaeologists to collect and archive the scrolls. This discovery has proven the current version of the Old Testament has not been altered to fit anyone's idea of history – it is the unchanged Word of God. Also, many of the scrolls were written hundreds of years before Jesus' ministry, so the prophecies of Jesus serve as verifiable proof of God's existence: Info On The Dead Sea Scrolls.[7]

Skeptics also thought that the Bible was proven to be wrong because it mentioned a nation of people called, Hittites, and there was no known evidence of their existence. Scientists and skeptics pointed to this to show the fictitious nature of the Bible. It caused many to turn their backs on God and the Bible, *Gen 15:18-21, "In the same day the Lord made a covenant with Abram, saying, Unto thy seed have I given this land, from the river of Egypt unto the great river, the river Euphrates: The Kenites, and the Kenizzites, and the Kadmonites, And the Hittites, and the Perizzites, and the Rephaims, And the Amorites, and the Canaanites, and the Girgashites, and the Jebusites."* These verses were written around 1430 BC. Some three thousand years later, in 1884, archaeological evidence finally proved the Bible was correct. William Wright found a monument with script mentioning the Hittites. And in 1906 Hugo Winckler found a royal archive containing 10,000 tablets, at what was the ancient city of Boğazköy, which has been identified as the capital of the Hittites. Science has an every changing opinion on every subject and that opinion will eventually come to agree with everything the Bible has told us, as it has so many times in the past.

Skeptics doubted the story of the walls just falling down in Jericho, *Josh 6:20, "So the people shouted when the priests blew with the trumpets: and it came to pass, when the people heard the sound of the trumpet, and the people shouted with a great shout, that the wall fell down flat, so that the people went up into the city, every man straight before him, and they took the city."* Archaeologists have been studying the site of ancient Jericho since Ernst Sellin and Carl Watzinger first began to work the site in 1907. The results of these studies have at one point confirmed the Bible account, at another point discounted it, and then again confirmed it. Currently it is on the confirming side of the argument, even though the skeptics now claim it was an earthquake. Of course, they will not admit that God could cause an earthquake. Ultimately, I am confident the Bible gave us an accurate account of the event. For more detailed discussion on this topic: Biblical Jericho Archaeological Evidence.[8] Would not an earthquake at that moment in time and place on earth, with the exact force necessary to cause the walls to fall flat be a rather amazing coincidence?

There are too many examples of fulfilled prophecy to fit into this book, however, I can refer you to an article for further study on the subject: Bible Prophecy Fulfilled.[9]

God has provided us the truth of His plan and told us how we can use that truth to live the best possible life. It is up to each of us to decide whether we will believe His Truth, *Rom 10:17, "So then faith cometh by hearing, and hearing by the word of God."* When we read the Bible we begin to hear the Word of God and discover His prophecies fulfilled and the truth of His message on how to live the best life. Then, we gain the faith necessary to reason with God in all areas of our lives. We can begin to reason with God without faith, however, eventually we will hear His Word, which will lead us to faith and the Truth. This is how I began my conversion, first I read the Bible with a heart looking for proof of either His existence or the lack thereof. It turns out the proof is overwhelming!

Acts 4:19, "But Peter and John answered and said unto them, Whether it be right in the sight of God to hearken unto you more than unto God, judge ye." Peter and John drive us to consider the foolishness of this world and the voices of the people trying to hearken unto us to follow a way other than God's way. How can we follow these confused or lying voices? They are rooted in selfishness and carry a message that is constantly changing to fit their current needs. God's message is the Truth and it never changes, *Jam 5:12, "But above all things, my brethren, swear not, neither by heaven, neither by the earth, neither by any other oath: but let your yea be yea; and your nay, nay; lest ye fall into condemnation."* God tells us His way is being truthful in all situations. He wants us to always tell the truth, even when it leads others to dislike us, even when it leads others to kill us. God knows this is not the easy path, which is why He tells us to persist through the tribulations we will face.

Can we look to our world full of addictions to prove God exists? Addictions come from the devil, because God will not tempt any man, *Jam 1:12-13, "Blessed is the man that endureth temptation: for when he is tried, he shall receive the crown of life, which the Lord hath promised to them that love him. Let no man say when he is tempted, I am tempted of God: for God cannot be tempted with evil, neither tempteth he any man:"* When we turn to God, He is faithful and shows us the way to escape our addictions, *1 Cor 10:13, "There hath no temptation taken you but such as is common to man: but God is faithful, who will not suffer you to be tempted above that ye are able; but will with the temptation also make a way to escape, that ye may be able to bear it."* Once the devil lures us into one addiction, he uses it to add additional addictions. It is as if each addiction is yet another chain that binds us to him. Slavery to him is his goal and only God can help us escape, *1 Cor 6:12, "All things are lawful unto me, but all things are not expedient: all things are lawful for me, but I will not be brought under the power of any."* Once we accept Jesus as our savior, we will have the power to resist future temptations, *Rom 6:6, "Knowing this, that our old man is crucified with him, that the body of sin might be destroyed, that henceforth we should not serve sin."* God told us many would not accept His way; this world proves God's existence by the number of people who turn to God and are able to resist their addictions and how others remain addicted while denying God's existence. The second step in the A.A. 12 Step Program is belief in a higher Power: <u>The 12 Steps.</u>[10]

God's prophecies for these last days provide further evidence of His existence. God wants us to be selfless, not selfish, *Lk 9:23, "And he said to them all, If any man will come after me, let him deny himself, and take up his cross daily, and follow me."* He has told us, *Acts 20:35, "I have shewed you all things, how that so labouring ye ought to support the weak, and to remember the words of the Lord Jesus, how he said, It is more blessed to give than to receive."* Because, *Jam 3:16, "For where envying and strife is, there is confusion and every evil work."* As it is in these last days, *2 Tim 3:1-4, "This know also, that in the last days perilous times shall come. For men shall be lovers of their own selves, covetous, boasters, proud, blasphemers, disobedient to parents, unthankful, unholy, Without natural affection, trucebreakers, false accusers, incontinent, fierce, despisers of those that are good, Traitors, heady, high-minded, lovers of pleasures more than lovers of God;"* God wants us to be the light shining in these last days, He wants us to care for others, *Rom 15:1-3, "We then that are strong ought to bear the infirmities of the weak, and not to please ourselves. Let every one of us please his neighbour for his good to edification. For even Christ pleased not himself; but, as it is written, The reproaches of them that reproached thee fell on me."* He will take their reproaches for us.

Dr. Michael Youssef wants us to understand the gift of prophecy God tells us about in the Bible: "Although speaking about events in the future is related to the gift of prophecy, Christians must make sure that what they believe about prophecy lines up with God's Word. The word prophecy is composed of two words that mean "forth" and "telling." "Forth telling" is very different from foretelling or predicting the future. Any Christian can speak forth what he knows to be true about the past, present, or future when his foundation for Truth is the Word of God, as revealed in the Bible. In writing the Scriptures, God gave authority and inspiration through the Holy Spirit to a group of prophets and apostles to record His Truth as the Holy Word, and then He closed the book. No one can add or subtract from what God has included in His Word. The source of prophecy today is the Bible. Anyone who speaks anything that is inconsistent with the Truth expressed in His Word is not speaking for God." Michael Youssef, Ph.D., is the founder of Leading The Way's International Ministries: http://www.ltw.org.[11] Dr. Youssef wants us to know God's Word will lead us to make good decisions and when we honestly use the prophecies of the Bible to lead others to God, His light will shine and people will follow that light.

Once we read the Biblical truths and prophecies, we are left with a decision. Either we believe the writers of the Old Testament were guided by God, that what they wrote has never changed, that the majority of the writers of the New Testament lived with Jesus until His death and resurrection, and that they then spent the rest of their lives preaching His Truth until they were martyred. Or, a big bang occurred spontaneously out of nothing, causing the evolution of this beautiful universe, which includes our planet; that simple life forms crawled out of a primordial ooze on our planet, which somehow created itself, and that these simple life forms, through evolution, developed into what we now know as humans and everything else we see.

If there is a God, who is He? Maybe, we can learn something from His many names. One of the meanings of my given name, William, is "desire to protect." Some might think that is a fitting name for me, especially since I have spent the past 40+ years in the insurance business, protecting people against the risks of everyday life. This name comes from the Germanic name Willahelm, which was composed of the elements wil "will, desire" and helm "helmet, protection" – from behindthename.com

We name our children after past family members, or give them names we like, or names that speak to our hope for our child's future, or some equally random thought process. As we go through life we get additional names from other sources like friends, co-workers, etc., names such as "red" or "doc." But, God's names describe who He is, what He is capable of doing, and what He has already done. Some of those names require that we read from the original text, so that we do not lose part of Him in translation.

Please pardon the lack of appropriate diacritics for the Hebrew, Greek & Aramaic words.

Gen 1:1, "In the beginning God created the heaven and the earth." In the original text, the word for "God" used in this verse is "Elohim" or "Elohiym," which means "creator." Or, as Socrates would have said, "first mover." Apparently, the first thing He wants us to know is that He creates, *Mk 10:6, "But from the beginning of the creation God made them male and female."*

Gen 16:13, "And she called the name of the Lord that spake unto her, Thou God seest me: for she said, Have I also here looked after him that seeth me?" In the original text, the word for "God" used in this verse is, "El Roi" or "El Roiy," which means "God Sees." He sees and knows everything we do. *Job 33:21, "For his eyes are upon the ways of man, and he seeth all his goings."*

Gen 22:14, "And Abraham called the name of that place Jehovahjireh: as it is said to this day, In the mount of the Lord it shall be seen." In the original text, the word for the "place Jehovahireh" used in this verse is, "Yahwe-Yire," which means "The Lord Will Provide." He is the provider of all that we need. *Matt 6:33, "But seek ye first the kingdom of God, and his righteousness; and all these things shall be added unto you."* and *Phil 4:19, "But my God shall supply all your need according to his riches in glory by Christ Jesus."*

Gen 17:1, "And when Abram was ninety years old and nine, the Lord appeared to Abram, and said unto him, I am the Almighty God; walk before me, and be thou perfect." In the original text, the word for "Almighty God" used in this verse is, "El Shaddai," "shaDay," or "Sadday," which means "Omnipotent." Since, God is Almighty, He can do anything. *Matt 19:26, "But Jesus beheld them, and said unto them, With men this is impossible; but with God all things are possible."*

Gen 21:33, "And Abraham planted a grove in Beersheba, and called there on the name of the Lord, the everlasting God." In the original text, the word for "the everlasting God" used in this verse is, "El Olam," which means "God Everlasting." God is telling us He is eternal; has always been, is, and will always be. *Rom 1:20, "For the invisible things of him from the creation of the world are clearly seen, being understood by the things that are made, even his eternal power and Godhead; so that they are without excuse".*

Ex 3:14, "And God said unto Moses, I Am That I Am: and he said, Thus shalt thou say unto the children of Israel, I Am hath sent me unto you." In the original text, the word for "I Am" used in this verse is "Hayah" (haw-yaw), which means "to be, or to exist." God told Moses His name is "I Am"; apparently, God wants us to know He exists, for without this belief there is no hope of salvation. *Heb 11:6, "But without faith it is impossible to please him: for he that cometh to God must believe that he is, and that he is a rewarder of them that diligently seek him."*

Ex 15:26, "And said, If thou wilt diligently hearken to the voice of the Lord thy God, and wilt do that which is right in his sight, and wilt give ear to his commandments, and keep all his statutes, I will put none of these diseases upon thee, which I have brought upon the Egyptians: for I am the

Lord that healeth thee." In the original text, the word for "the Lord that healeth thee" used in this verse is, "Yahwe-Rofeca" or "Yahweh-Rapha," which means "The Lord Who Heals." He provides healing for both the body and the soul. *Gen 20:17, "So Abraham prayed unto God: and God healed Abimelech, and his wife, and his maidservants; and they bare children."* and *Matt 12:15 "But when Jesus knew it, he withdrew himself from thence: and great multitudes followed him, and he healed them all"*.

Judg 6:22, "And when Gideon perceived that he was an angel of the Lord, Gideon said, Alas, O Lord God! for because I have seen an angel of the Lord face to face." In the original text, the word for "God" used in this verse is, "YHWH," "Yahwe," "Yahweh," and the word for "Lord" is "Adonai" or "adonay." The written name is usually YHWH, but when reading the Jews did not want to say His name aloud for fear they might somehow misuse it, so they said "Adonai" instead. This is normally connotes a "Master" or a "Sovereign Ruler." *Matt 22:37, "Jesus said unto him, Thou shalt love the Lord thy God with all thy heart, and with all thy soul, and with all thy mind."*

Judg 6:24, "Then Gideon built an altar there unto the Lord, and called it Jehovahshalom: unto this day it is yet in Ophrah of the Abiezrites." In the original text, the word for "Jehowahshalom" used in this verse is, "Yahwe-Salom" or "Yahweh-Shalom," which means "The Lord Our Peace." He is the Prince of Peace, the "Sar-Shalom." *Is 9:6, "For unto us a child is born, unto us a son is given: and the government shall be upon his shoulder: and his name shall be called Wonderful, Counsellor, The mighty God, The everlasting Father, The Prince of Peace."*

Ps 23:1, "The Lord is my shepherd; I shall not want." In the original text, the word for "shepherd" used in this verse is, "Y'hwah roiy," "Yaweh Ro i," or "Yahweh-Rohi," which means, "shepherd" or "guide." *Ps 119:105, "Thy word is a lamp unto my feet, and a light unto my path."* and *Matt 16:24, "Then said Jesus unto his disciples, If any man will come after me, let him deny himself, and take up his cross, and follow me."* and *Rom 2:4, "Or despisest thou the riches of his goodness and forbearance and longsuffering; not knowing that the goodness of God leadeth thee to repentance?"*

Jer 23:23, "Am I a God at hand, saith the Lord, and not a God afar off?" In the original text, the word for "God at hand" used in this verse is "Elohey miQarov" or "Elohim qarowb," which means "God that is near." God is everywhere, He is not a distant God that cares little for His creation, He is always nearby, and He is part of all things. *Col 1:16, "And he is before all things, and by him all things consist."*

Jer 33:16, "In those days shall Judah be saved, and Jerusalem shall dwell safely: and this is the name wherewith she shall be called, The Lord our righteousness." In the original text, the word for "The Lord our righteousness" used in this verse is, "Y'hwah-tzid'qenu s" or "Yahwe-Xiokenu," which means "The Lord Our Righteousness." *2 Cor 5:21, "For he hath made him to be sin for us, who knew no sin; that we might be made the righteousness of God in him."* and *1 Pet 1:16, "Because it is written, Be ye holy; for I am holy."*

Mal 3:6, "For I am the Lord, I change not; therefore ye sons of Jacob are not consumed." In the original text, the word for "I change not" used in this verse is "shaniytiy", or "shanah lo", which means "immutable." God never changes, the same yesterday, today, and for all eternity. *Heb 13:8, "Jesus Christ the same yesterday, and to day, and for ever."*

Rom 8:15, "For ye have not received the spirit of bondage again to fear; but ye have received the Spirit of adoption, whereby we cry, Abba, Father." "Abba, Father" is an Aramaic utterance within the original Greek text, it is the name Jesus uses when He calls to God and the Aramaic words used in this verse are, "abba o pathr", which implies an intimate relationship and means "Father." Jesus is telling us that God is our Father and we can have the same intimate relationship with God by accepting Jesus as our savior. Jesus would be our brother and God the Father would be our Father. *Matt 12:50, "For whosoever shall do the will of my Father which is in heaven, the same is my brother, and sister, and mother."*

So, *who* is He? He is a living, all-powerful creator, who is eternal, never changing, a loving Father, who is everywhere, sees everything, ruler of everything, completely righteous, a guide, a provider, the Prince of Peace, and the ultimate healer. And, He loves us unconditionally.

What is God Like?

God's nature is demonstrated by what He thinks, says, feels and does.

God is love and that influences everything, *1 Jn 4:8, 16, "He that loveth not knoweth not God; for God is love. And we have known and believed the love that God hath to us. God is love; and he that dwelleth in love dwelleth in God, and God in him."* God is telling us He dwells in love, which means He thinks it, He says it, He feels it, and He lives it.

Since true love is selfless, God is selfless and He is always working for the good of others, *1 Cor 13:4-5, "Charity suffereth long, and is kind; charity envieth not; charity vaunteth not itself, is not puffed up, Doth not behave itself unseemly, seeketh not her own, is not easily provoked, thinketh no evil;"* Everything God thinks, says, feels and does is for the benefit of the eternal family He is creating.

He loves each of us, *Jn 11:35-36, "Jesus wept. Then said the Jews, Behold how he loved him!"* Jesus cares about everyone who is suffering and all of those who have died, He cares to the point of tears. He weeps for all, especially for those who will choose to reject Him.

God is merciful, gracious, and patient, *Ex34:6, "And the Lord passed by before him, and proclaimed, The Lord, The Lord God, merciful and gracious, longsuffering, and abundant in goodness and truth"* He is patient and allows us to struggle and fight against His plan, while at the same time allowing us the choice to accept or reject His offer of salvation, no matter how many times we have previously rejected it. This freedom He gives us means He has to watch us fall and suffer the pain that will surely result, without restricting our freedom. Now that takes patience. What God experiences in this process is like our watching our own child learning to walk, there will be falls.

God does not lie and He always keeps His promises, *Numb 23:19, "God is not a man, that he should lie; neither the son of man, that he should repent: hath he said, and shall he not do it? Or hath he spoken, and shall he not make it good?"* God shares His Truth with us, in the form of promises, which He guarantees will come to pass. We can depend on everything He tells us. This includes the best way to live our lives.

God believes in fairness, and this requires a rule of law firmly rooted in love, *Matt 22:35-40, "Then one of them, which was a lawyer, asked him a question, tempting him, and saying, Master, which is the great commandment in the law? Jesus said unto him, Thou shalt love the Lord thy God with all thy heart, and with all thy soul, and with all thy mind. This is the first and great commandment. And the second is like unto it, Thou shalt love thy neighbour as thyself. On these two commandments hang all the law and the prophets."* and *Rom 13:10, "Love worketh no ill to his neighbour: therefore love is the fulfilling of the law."* When we all truly love everyone, there will be no need for laws.

God will always love us, no matter what, *Rom 8:35, 38-39, "Who shall separate us from the love of Christ? Shall tribulation, or distress, or persecution, or famine, or nakedness, or peril, or sword? For I am persuaded, that neither death, nor life, nor angels, nor principalities, nor powers, nor things present, nor things to come, nor height, nor depth, nor any other creature, shall be able to separate us from the love of God, which is in Christ Jesus our Lord."* Study the way He describes a father's love in the prodigal son: Lk 15:11-32.[12] The father's nature is to love and always accept his son, as God does us. All we have to do is return to Him and we will feel the love He has always had for us, *Rev 3:20, "Behold, I stand at the door, and knock: if any man hear my voice, and open the door, I will come in to him, and will sup with him, and he with me."* He is always ready to sup with those who open the door. When we refuse to open the door, our guilt keeps us from feeling His love for us and activates the defense mechanism of thinking He does not exist. For, if He did exist, all that we do in defiance of His Word would become obvious. Therefore, we have to try to hide from His existence, which is impossible, *Gen 3:9, "And the Lord God called unto Adam, and said unto him, Where art thou?"* He asked Adam where he was, but we all know God already knew where Adam was.

God is benevolent. He has the ultimate power and uses it to give us every chance to learn the Truth and accept His offer of grace, *Jer 32:17, "Ah Lord God! Behold, thou hast made the heaven and the earth by thy great power and stretched out arm, and there is nothing too hard for thee:"* and *Ps 145:8, "The Lord is gracious, and full of compassion; slow to anger, and of great mercy."* He could kill us, but instead He continually offers us His love. No other being, with this kind of great power, has used it for the ultimate good, all the time. This is true because no other being is God.

God's love extends to everyone, *Matt 5:44-45, "But I say unto you, Love your enemies, bless them that curse you, do good to them that hate you, and pray for them which despitefully use you, and persecute you; That ye may be the children of your Father which is in heaven: for he maketh his sun to rise on the evil and on the good, and sendeth rain on the just and on the unjust."* The nature of God demonstrated in these verses is the reason we sinners are able to come to Him, knowing that He will always accept us. These verses also explain why He allows those He knows will not accept His offer to continue to exist. This gives us the understanding we need, when we see the unjust receiving the sun and the rain, it keeps us from being drawn away from God's love. He gave us His tenth Commandment to keep us from the evil of envy, *Ex 20:17, "Thou shalt not covet thy neighbour's house, thou shalt not covet thy neighbour's wife, nor his manservant, nor his maidservant, nor his ox, nor his ass, nor any thing that is thy neighbour's."* He still wants those who live in defiance of His love to have every opportunity to change their minds, so that they will be without excuse for the choices they have made. For a better understanding of the principle in play here, see the parable of the wheat and the tares: <u>*Matt 13:18-30*</u>.[13]

We could go on for pages talking about God's nature and love for us. However, the most powerful proof of His love is the way His love changes people's lives. I have seen drug dealers became elders in churches, drug addicts in recovery, and ordinary people like me busily removing sin and selfishness from our lives. We do not have to look too far to find these examples; God has placed witnesses in every community, even prisons. To personally experience His love we only have to open the door, feel His love and see salvation transform our lives.

God is reasonable because He reasons before He acts. He tries to teach us to do the same, *Is 1:18, "Come now, and let us reason together, saith the Lord: though your sins be as scarlet, they shall be as white as snow; though they be red like crimson, they shall be as wool."* He is teaching us in Isaiah that when we reason before we act, more and more of our actions will be good and we will continue to remove sin from our lives. Some might twinge when they read we can remove sin from our lives, however, they have not read, *2 Tim 3:16-17, "All scripture is given by inspiration of God, and is profitable for doctrine, for reproof, for correction, for instruction in righteousness: That the man of God may be perfect, thoroughly furnished unto all good works."* Perfect is possible, but I am not sure how much time I will have to spend reading and reasoning with God to get there. Or, maybe some of us are not meant to achieve it in this life, but rather to understand what it looks like and work toward it, *Rom 3:23, "For all have sinned, and come short of the glory of God;"* Only Jesus lived a perfect life, but have some reached perfection during their lives on Earth?

How are we created in the image of God? God has three parts and so we have three parts, a mind (cognitive), a spirit (spiritual) and a body (physical), as Peter explains in, *1 Pet 1:1-2, "Peter, an apostle of Jesus Christ, to the strangers scattered throughout Pontus,*

Galatia, Cappadocia, Asia, and Bithynia, Elect according to the foreknowledge of God the Father, through sanctification of the Spirit, unto obedience and sprinkling of the blood of Jesus Christ: Grace unto you, and peace, be multiplied." Peter is identifying himself as an elect. An elect is one who opened the door when Jesus knocked, known by the mind of God before he was born, the cognitive; by sanctification of the Holy Spirit, the spiritual; and saved unto obedience because of the physical blood of Christ Jesus, the physical.

"God the Father" is the cognitive part of God. Jesus explains how this works, *Jn 5:19, "Then answered Jesus and said unto them, Verily, verily, I say unto you, The Son can do nothing of himself, but what he seeth the Father do: for what things soever he doeth, these also doeth the Son likewise."* God gave us minds to be our cognitive part. He gave us minds so that He could reason with us, to help us understand His plan, so we could have the necessary cognitive power to make a decision to believe or not, and to provide a way for us to learn how to complete our part in His plan, if we decide that is what we want. He does not want robots worshipping Him; He wants a family who reasons and chooses to love each other, *Is 1:18, "Come now, and let us reason together, saith the Lord: though your sins be as scarlet, they shall be as white as snow; though they be red like crimson, they shall be as wool."*

This mind, "God the Father," is difficult for us to imagine, for we have limited minds and imaginations. However, this mind knows all, past, present and future; understands all, everything that ever was and everything that will ever be; created everything, first by imagining it, then willing it into existence, *Acts 15:18, "Known unto God are all his works from the beginning of the world."* God knew what He was going to do before He even began to create. What chance is there that we humans could somehow know better? *Prov 21:30, "There is no wisdom nor understanding nor counsel against the Lord."*

Our world is madly racing toward the day we can claim we have no need of God. We continue to press toward the day that we can say we have replaced Him. One step in this process is the creating of A. I.: artificial intelligence. We believe we can create a computer that will be better than the mind God created for us. But, a mind independent from God will not seek the same results. This artificial intelligence will be cold and calculating. Humanity and the love that is God will not be part of this computer. A.I. is incapable of the relationships God is creating, *Dan 5:13-14, "Then was Daniel brought in before the king. And the king spake and said unto Daniel, Art thou that Daniel, which art of the children of the captivity of Judah, whom the king my father brought out of Jewry? I have even heard of thee, that the spirit of the gods is in thee, and that light and understanding and excellent wisdom is found in thee."* The king was amazed at the excellent wisdom he heard was in Daniel. The king knew it was from God, because it was different from anything he had experienced before in his godless world. Notice how the same thing happened to Jesus, *Matt 13:54, "And when he was come into his own country, he taught them in their synagogue, insomuch that they were astonished, and said, Whence hath this man this wisdom, and these mighty works?"* The religious leaders of Jesus' day could not believe that a twelve-year-old boy could bring the words of God, which they had been studying their whole lives, to life in a way that showed God's love. Hear how James describes Jesus' message: *Jam 3:17, "But the wisdom that is from above is first pure, then peaceable, gentle, and easy to be intreated, full of mercy and good fruits, without partiality, and without hypocrisy."* Our world is corrupt; this is why we need to understand how reasoning with God can change everything in our lives. There is no corruption in God, so nothing in this world can come against the Word of God and prevail, *1 Jn 1:5, "This then is the message which we have heard of him, and declare unto you, that God is light, and in him is no darkness at all."*

Without God, our minds are free to think themselves wise enough to play with evil, which leads to our undoing, *Prov 3:7, "Be not wise in thine own eyes: fear the Lord, and depart from evil."* For only God can help us understand the difference between good and evil, thus allowing us to freely choose good. This understanding comes from our minds reasoning with "God the Father," cognitive conscience to cognitive conscience.

Ps 10:4, "The wicked, through the pride of his countenance, will not seek after God: God is not in all his thoughts." Pride can separate us from the wisdom of God, because pride prevents us from reasoning with Him. We therefore waste the precious gift He offers. God wants us to lay down our pride, *Eze 16:49, "Behold, this was the iniquity of thy sister Sodom, pride, fulness of bread, and abundance of idleness was in her and in her daughters, neither did she strengthen the hand of the poor and needy."* God warns us that our pride will cause us to do evil things, *Job 35:12, "There they cry, but none giveth answer, because of the pride of evil men."* God tells us that the prideful will not seek Him, therefore, they will not find His wisdom, *Prov 11:2, 13:10, "When pride cometh, then cometh shame: but with the lowly is wisdom…Only by pride cometh contention: but with the well advised is wisdom."* God tells us that our pride leads to a haughty spirit, which leads to our fall, *Prov 16:18, "Pride goeth before destruction, and an haughty spirit before a fall."* Ultimately, He wants us to know that pride does not come from God, *1 Jn 2:16, "For all that is in the world, the lust of the flesh, and the lust of the eyes, and the pride of life, is not of the Father, but is of the world."*

Ps 14:1, "The fool hath said in his heart, There is no God. They are corrupt, they have done abominable works, there is none that doeth good." Those who believe there is a God, reason with Him, which leads them to follow His commandments. These people are not perfect, yet. However, because they believe, when they break a commandment they feel it weighing down their conscience. The "fool" feels the weight, but does not know what it means. This very fact leads many to contemplate suicide, or seek drugs, for they see no other way out of this feeling. Others that refuse to accept God tend to look to their own wisdom to solve their problems, rather than the Word of God. The heart of the matter is whether we are willing to reason with God. When we are humble enough to seek His guidance, to try to understand His will for us, we will always find it in His Word, *Jam 1:5, "If any of you lack wisdom, let him ask of God, that giveth to all men liberally, and upbraideth not; and it shall be given him."* He giveth to all men liberally. Our choice is whether we will accept His gift, or not.

Col 1:15, "Who is the image of the invisible God, the firstborn of every creature:" Pure thought is invisible to us. Of course, this problem has led us to thinking we can see pure thought on a computer screen. Unless we are reading the Word of God on that computer screen, we are not interacting with "God the Father." When we reason with God, we are allowing our minds to communicate directly with the mind of "God the Father." The fact that we cannot see His mind does not change the fact that He exists.

1 Cor 1:20-21, "Where is the wise? Where is the scribe? Where is the disputer of this world? Hath not God made foolish the wisdom of this world? For after that in the wisdom of God the world by wisdom knew not God, it pleased God by the foolishness of preaching to save them that believe." God knows that those who think themselves too wise to believe in God will not listen when someone is preaching the gospel to them. He knows that they certainly will not take the time to reason with Him, *Heb 11:6, "But without faith it is impossible to please him: for he that cometh to God must believe that he is, and that he is a rewarder of them that diligently seek him."* We cannot pretend to believe and still reason with God. Going through the motions of reasoning with God will not bring change. This is the problem the Pharisees had. Only true belief will lead to genuine reasoning, which allows us to begin the transformation process, which leads to change. This is why wise men will be ashamed when they face judgment, *Jer 8:9, "The wise men are ashamed, they are dismayed and*

taken: lo, they have rejected the word of the Lord; and what wisdom is in
them?"

"God the Father" has seen all things, past, present and future.
Jesus is our example. He does the will of the Father, every time, *Jn
4:34, "Jesus saith unto them, My meat is to do the will of him that sent me,
and to finish his work."* When we follow Jesus' example, we will
surely choose to do the will of the Father in this life.

*Is 48:5, "I have even from the beginning declared it to thee; before it
came to pass I shewed it thee: lest thou shouldest say, Mine idol hath done
them, and my graven image, and my molten image, hath commanded
them."* Knowing that we humans exaggerate to elevate our own
image, God declared the future to prevent the misuse of history.
Those who would claim to have done something that God has done,
would not only look foolish, but would eventually be seen as
frauds. We will know these frauds by their fruits, *Matt 7:20,
"Wherefore by their fruits ye shall know them."*

*1 Cor 3:19, "For the wisdom of this world is foolishness with God. For
it is written, He taketh the wise in their own craftiness."* Knowing the
future, God has created this world in a way that allows for humans
to seem wise. Ultimately, they will be proven foolish. This has
already happened so many times it is impossible to challenge this
bit of wisdom, here are but a few examples of man's wisdom
proven to be foolishness: The Earth is flat; Wilhelm Reich's thought
he discovered orgone; Focal Infection Theory resulted in millions of
people being subjected to needless dental extractions and surgeries;
the Clovis First theory was finally discredited; the Earth as the

center of the universe; Miasmatic Theory of disease as a result of bad air was debunked; immovable continents was disproved in the middle of the 19th century; the four humours of Hippocratic medicine were black bile, yellow bile, phlegm and blood was finally disproved; the theory of spontaneous generation was popular for well over a thousand years; Phlogiston was an element believed to exist in all things that burned; Plato believed that light emanated from the eye; bloodletting was a prevalent practice for over 2,000 years; the idea of the Pythagoreans that all numbers can be expressed as a ratio of two whole numbers was disproved by one of Pythagoras' own disciples; a "theorem" of Jan-Erik Roos in 1961 stated that in an [AB4*] abelian category, lim vanishes on Mittag-Leffler sequences, but it was disproved by counterexample in 2002 by Amnon Neeman; and Rogue waves were considered myths by science until 1995. We could keep adding to this list forever. Here is one who expresses what God has told us all along, in 1967 Francis Crick, the co-discoverer of the structure of DNA, stated, "And so to those of you who may be vitalists I would make this prophecy: what everyone believed yesterday, and you believe today, only cranks will believe tomorrow."

The point is: only one mind knows all and has created everything by willing the completion of His plan, "God the Father." While we spend our time trying to prove something independent of God, He asks us to believe and help Him create His eternal family. He calls us to do this by completing our part in His plan, instead of trying to prove how smart we are.

The Holy Spirit is the spiritual part of God. The Spirit and the soul: What are they and how are they different?

Gen 2:7, "And the Lord God formed man of the dust of the ground, and breathed into his nostrils the breath of life; and man became a living soul." Man became a living soul when God breathed the breath of life into his nostrils. If souls can be living, what else can they be? What is the breath of life?

Job 33:4, "The spirit of God hath made me, and the breath of the Almighty hath given me life." When we combine the Holy Spirit with the mind and the body God has given us, we become a living soul. Only God can kill the soul. *Gen 25:8, "Then Abraham gave up the ghost, and died in a good old age, an old man, and full of years; and was gathered to his people."* When Abraham gave up the ghost, his unique spiritual part of God was separated from his mind and body. His body was now dead, but what happened to his soul?

Rev 6:9, "And when he had opened the fifth seal, I saw under the altar the souls of them that were slain for the word of God, and for the testimony which they held:" When those who can kill the body have completed their ugly deed, the unique spiritual part of God that is needed to create our soul returns to God. However, that part of us is without a mind and body, so it is in what we would call a state of suspended animation. Or, as the Bible calls it, sleep; *Lk 8:52, "And all wept, and bewailed her: but he said, Weep not; she is not dead, but sleepeth."* and *Ps 13:3, "Consider and hear me, O Lord my God: lighten mine eyes, lest I sleep the sleep of death;"*

This spiritual part of us has the potential of eternal life. Each of us must decide for ourselves, do we want to live eternally, or do we want this life to be the end. Only by refusing to accept God's offer and the spiritual part He breathed into our nostrils, do we lose this eternal life, *Matt 12:31-32, "Wherefore I say unto you, All manner of sin and blasphemy shall be forgiven unto men: but the blasphemy against the Holy Ghost shall not be forgiven unto men. And whosoever speaketh a word against the Son of man, it shall be forgiven him: but whosoever speaketh against the Holy Ghost, it shall not be forgiven him, neither in this world, neither in the world to come."* Denying the Holy Spirit is like holding our breath. There is a limit to it and then we die. It is interesting to think that we can live without food for 3 weeks, sleep 11 days, water 4 days, but air only 5 minutes. Apparently, there is something to this breath of life stuff.

When our unique part of God's Spirit is united with a mind and a body, it awakens from its sleep to become what we would call alive, *1 Thes 3:15-16, "For this we say unto you by the word of the Lord, that we which are alive and remain unto the coming of the Lord shall not prevent them which are asleep. For the Lord himself shall descend from heaven with a shout, with the voice of the archangel, and with the trump of God: and the dead in Christ shall rise first:"* and *1 Cor 14:52, "In a moment, in the twinkling of an eye, at the last trump: for the trumpet shall sound, and the dead shall be raised incorruptible, and we shall be changed."* When Jesus returns, the dead shall rise incorruptible, an immortal mind and body will unite with our unique part of God's Spirit, and we again become a living soul and awake to eternal life.

Ps 19:7, "The law of the Lord is perfect, converting the soul: the testimony of the Lord is sure, making wise the simple." What does converting the soul mean? *Acts 6:3, "Wherefore, brethren, look ye out among you seven men of honest report, full of the Holy Ghost and wisdom, whom we may appoint over this business."* When we are full of the Holy Ghost and accept the wisdom of God, we are converted. To put it simply, we accept the love of God. This is when we become agents of love. Love, it is an interesting word. God keeps it simple; He tells us that love is selfless. We will know when someone is full of the Holy Ghost, and wisdom, for we will see the fruits in their actions. Increasingly they care more about others than they do about themselves. They are becoming selfless.

The Holy Ghost lives in each of us. When we deny Him, we are unable to hear His voice. The closer we come to God and His will for us, the louder the voice of the Holy Ghost gets, *Is 48:16, "Come ye near unto me, hear ye this; I have not spoken in secret from the beginning; from the time that it was, there am I: and now the Lord God, and his Spirit, hath sent me."* When we begin to listen to the Holy Spirit, as Isaiah did, God is able to tell us about our part in His plan. He then sends us into the world to be His messengers. We just need to turn up the volume by moving closer to God.

Jesus is the physical part of God, or what we might call the body, *Jn 20:17, 21, 27, "Jesus saith unto her, Touch me not; for I am not yet ascended to my Father: but go to my brethren, and say unto them, I ascend unto my Father, and your Father; and to my God, and your God... Then said Jesus to them again, Peace be unto you: as my Father hath sent*

47

me, even so send I you… Then saith he to Thomas, Reach hither thy finger, and behold my hands; and reach hither thy hand, and thrust it into my side: and be not faithless, but believing." When Jesus was resurrected He was in spirit form and would not let Mary touch Him. After He had ascended and returned from God, He allowed Thomas to touch Him. He was no longer in spirit form, but a spirit in a physical body. He wants us to learn from this experience, to gain faith from it.

Jesus tells us that He follows the will of the Father. He is not making things up as He goes. He is the body that acts according to the will of the Father, *Jn 4:24, "Jesus saith unto them, My meat is to do the will of him that sent me, and to finish his work."* Jesus is our example and He is showing us that our bodies do what our minds will; and that is why we are to reason with God the Father by reading His Word and following the example of the Living Word He sent to us, before we act. Only then can we understand and follow God's will for our lives. Jesus is telling us that all He does is the fulfillment of the will of the Father. A choice.

Jesus Himself told us that only the Father knows when Jesus will return, *Matt 24:36, "But of that day and hour knoweth no man, no, not the angels of heaven, but my Father only."* It is the Father that knows all and gives directions to those willing to follow His plan, even Jesus.

Jesus is our example, the sacrifice, the only way for us to live in this body and still be saved, *Jude 24-25, "Now unto him that is able to keep you from falling, and to present you faultless before the presence of his glory with exceeding joy, To the only wise God our Saviour, be glory and majesty, dominion and power, both now and ever. Amen."* When Jesus walked this Earth, those who really took the time to see Him, His nature and His miracles, knew He was God. They gave up everything on this Earth for the eternity He promises. They accepted Him as their savior and He strengthened them, so that they could resist the devil's temptations that would have led to their falling away from God. He showed us how to live by His example. He promised He would present us to God sinless, for He would die on the cross and take our sins with Him, *Matt 26:27-29, "And he took the cup, and gave thanks, and gave it to them, saying, Drink ye all of it; For this is my blood of the new testament, which is shed for many for the remission of sins. But I say unto you, I will not drink henceforth of this fruit of the vine, until that day when I drink it new with you in my Father's kingdom."* His blood was shed for many for the remission of their sins.

Jesus reminds us that we all fear the death of our bodies, to the point of sweating blood. But, He also shows us that following the will of our Father is the most important thing we will do. No matter what the cost, *Lk 22:41-44, "And he was withdrawn from them about a stone's cast, and kneeled down, and prayed, Saying, Father, if thou be willing, remove this cup from me: nevertheless not my will, but thine, be done. And there appeared an angel unto him from heaven, strengthening him. And being in an agony he prayed more earnestly: and his sweat was as it were great drops of blood falling down to the ground."* "He prayed more earnestly" as we should when we need strengthening.

Jesus wanted only to finish the work God the Father had given Him to do, *Jn 19:30*, *"When Jesus therefore had received the vinegar, he said, It is finished: and he bowed his head, and gave up the ghost."* Jesus completed His work, and then His body died. *Heb 9:28, "So Christ was once offered to bear the sins of many; and unto them that look for him shall he appear the second time without sin unto salvation."*

On the third day He walked out of the tomb and returned to His Father. Then, He came back to Earth to show His disciples, and many more, that He had risen from the grave and was now in His immortal body. He had conquered the first death for all of us, *Heb 2:9, "But we see Jesus, who was made a little lower than the angels for the suffering of death, crowned with glory and honour; that he by the grace of God should taste death for every man,"* for every person.

Therefore, we no longer need to fear those who threaten to kill the body. For, we know that we will be resurrected when Jesus returns, *1 Thes 4:16-17, "For the Lord himself shall descend from heaven with a shout, with the voice of the archangel, and with the trump of God: and the dead in Christ shall rise first: Then we which are alive and remain shall be caught up together with them in the clouds, to meet the Lord in the air: and so shall we ever be with the Lord."* We have not seen Jesus, yet. But, we can have faith, for those who saw Him before and after the first death have given us their lives as a testimony to the Truth, they are our witnesses, *Jn 15:27, "And ye also shall bear witness, because ye have been with me from the beginning."*

God gave us our bodies so that we might complete our part in His plan, as Moses demonstrates for us, *Ex 40:33, "And he reared up the court round about the tabernacle and the altar, and set up the hanging of the court gate. So Moses finished the work."* Saul was told he would become Paul and a great witness to all the world of the Truth of Jesus Christ, *Acts 22:14, "And he said, The God of our fathers hath chosen thee, that thou shouldest know his will, and see that Just One, and shouldest hear the voice of his mouth."* Moses and Saul are but two of the many who finished the work God willed for them.

Many of the things we do in this life are driven by our need to fulfill the wants of the body. But, when those things are in conflict with God's plan for our lives, we need to be willing to follow God's plan, His will, *Acts 4:19, "But Peter and John answered and said unto them, Whether it be right in the sight of God to hearken unto you more than unto God, judge ye."* Peter and John are telling us that we should always hearken to God. We should not let others or our own bodies control our actions. When we decide to follow God's plan for our lives, little by little, more of our actions will be in alignment with His plan. Patience is required.

His plan culminates in our joining our bodies with Christ. We become one body, which He calls His church. This is not an organized religion; it is a group of individuals, freely accepting the gift of salvation, *Rom 12:5, "So we, being many, are one body in Christ, and everyone members one of another."* We become one body, moving toward God. Just as we are not to have members of our own bodies warring, we members of the body of Christ should not war against each other, *1 Cor 12:12, "For as the body is one, and hath many members, and all the members of that one body, being many, are one body: so also is*

Christ." We all have work to do for the body Christ is building, just as individual parts of our bodies have different duties necessary to keep our bodies functioning. When enough of us do the work God wills for us, the body of Christ will be complete and Jesus will return to collect us.

When we complete the work God has willed for us, we will one day hear these words; *Matt 25:21, "His lord said unto him, Well done, thou good and faithful servant: thou hast been faithful over a few things, I will make thee ruler over many things: enter thou into the joy of thy lord."* God is joyfully waiting to say them to us.

Jesus is God and is man – that is the only way He could bridge the gap of sin between the two. He died as a man and took all of our sins with Him to the grave, *1 Tim 2:5, "For there is one God, and one mediator between God and men, the man Christ Jesus;"* Peter is talking to men who had witnessed for themselves the truth of the miracles Jesus performed, as a man and God. *Acts 2:22, "Ye men of Israel, hear these words; Jesus of Nazareth, a man approved of God among you by miracles and wonders and signs, which God did by him in the midst of you, as ye yourselves also know:"* Luke is pointing to Peter's words to help us know that they had all witnessed the miracles; and that we can have faith that Jesus is the Messiah spoken of in the Old Testament.

Jesus is the body of God and anyone who saw Him saw the Father, *Jn 14:9, "Jesus saith unto him, Have I been so long time with you, and yet hast thou not known me, Philip? He that hath seen me hath seen the Father; and how sayest thou then, Show us the Father?"* Jesus is telling us that He is the body of God, the Father. Who would know better?

Jesus is the image of the invisible God, the Father, *Col 1:15-18,* *"Who is the image of the invisible God, the firstborn of every creature: For by him were all things created, that are in heaven, and that are in earth, visible and invisible, whether they be thrones, or dominions, or principalities, or powers: all things were created by him, and for him: And he is before all things, and by him all things consist. And he is the head of the body, the church: who is the beginning, the firstborn from the dead; that in all things he might have the preeminence."* Jesus is the visible part of the invisible God: Jesus is the body of God.

When God sends us out into the world, He gives us all we need to complete our part in His plan, *Matt 10:19-20,* *"But when they deliver you up, take no thought how or what ye shall speak: for it shall be given you in that same hour what ye shall speak. For it is not ye that speak, but the Spirit of your Father which speaketh in you."* Even if we think we are not capable, we can have faith that the Holy Spirit will instruct us.

God has warned us that there would be people in the end times who will have separated themselves from the Spirit, they will be led by the lusts of the flesh, *Jude 17-23,* *"But, beloved, remember ye the words which were spoken before of the apostles of our Lord Jesus Christ; How that they told you there should be mockers in the last time, who should walk after their own ungodly lusts. These be they who separate themselves, sensual, having not the Spirit. But ye, beloved, building up yourselves on your most holy faith, praying in the Holy Ghost, Keep yourselves in the love of God, looking for the mercy of our Lord Jesus Christ unto eternal life. And of some have compassion, making a difference: And others save with fear, pulling them out of the fire; hating even the garment spotted by the flesh."* Notice that Jude is telling us to remember we are to keep ourselves in the love of God and show mercy to these end times people who have separated themselves. Only when they see God's love shining through us will they be able to find their way back to God and away from the second death. We cannot help these people with angry preaching. We will only drive them further towards our adversary, the devil, *Rev 2:7, "He that hath an ear, let him hear what the Spirit saith unto the churches; To him that overcometh will I give to eat of the tree of life, which is in the midst of the paradise of God."* God is telling us to listen to the Holy Spirit, so that "God the Father" can give us the eternal life He created for us.

How can we do this? By studying the Bible, praying and listening for the voice of the Holy Spirit, *Rom 5:1, 2, 8, "Therefore being justified by faith, we have peace with God through our Lord Jesus Christ: By whom also we have access by faith into this grace wherein we stand, and rejoice in hope of the glory of God... But God commendeth his love toward us, in that, while we were yet sinners, Christ died for us."* God is telling us that our faith allows us to have access to His grace. Our faith means we allow ourselves to reason with God. Reading the Bible allows us to decide whether we believe what we are reading. The Holy Spirit will teach us, if we allow Him to do His part, *1 Cor 2:13, "Which things also we speak, not in the words which man's wisdom teacheth, but which the Holy Ghost teacheth; comparing spiritual things with spiritual."* God continues to do His part. It is up to us to do our part – a choice, gently offered, hopefully given.

The Bible?

The Bible is a collection of books written by some 40 authors over a period of 1,500 years. How could 40 different writers spread over 1,500 years write such a cohesive work? They were being inspired by God, *2 Tim 3:16-17, "All scripture is given by inspiration of God, and is profitable for doctrine, for reproof, for correction, for instruction in righteousness: That the man of God may be perfect, thoroughly furnished unto all good works."* For those interested in doing good rather than evil, the Bible is the best "how to" source available.

But, to say it is only a collection of books would not be enough. The Bible is a love letter, a love letter from God to us. "The Bible is the only book where the author is in love with the reader." Author unknown, as seen on Pinterest. God has written this love letter to each of us. He is telling us that He will always love us, even if we refuse to accept His invitation to eternity. This is how much God loves each of us. When we read the Bible with this in mind, we begin to see His love pouring out of each page, *1 Jn 4:19, "We love him, because he first loved us."* and *Jn 3:16, "For God so loved the world, that he gave his only begotten Son, that whosoever believeth in him should not perish, but have everlasting life."*

Everything God teaches us is rooted in love, *Eph 5:25, "Husbands, love your wives, even as Christ also loved the church, and gave himself for it;"* This is how He tells men to treat their wives, love them as Christ has loved us, being ready and willing to give our lives for them. Sure, this means dying if that sacrifice will prevent our wives from dying, but it also means other sacrifices for them. Giving up that part of our lives that would lead us away from them, instead of toward the deeper love they deserve. God asks us to walk away from whatever is leading us away from our wives: drugs, gambling, adultery, entertainment, etc. How many divorces would there be if everyone treated their spouses the way God asks us to treat them?

Matt 5:43-46, "Ye have heard that it hath been said, Thou shalt love thy neighbour, and hate thine enemy. But I say unto you, Love your enemies, bless them that curse you, do good to them that hate you, and pray for them which despitefully use you, and persecute you; That ye may be the children of your Father which is in heaven: for he maketh his sun to rise on the evil and on the good, and sendeth rain on the just and on the unjust." God loves all of us and when we follow His advice, those who think themselves our enemies will see God's love in us. It will be God's love shining through us and it might be the first time they see His love. It might be the moment that changes their lives. I now understand the times I have experienced this lesson. Someone I was competing with for a spot on a team, or a place in a group, someone I perceived as my enemy, somehow miraculously transitioned into one of my best friends. I thought they were my adversaries, but I was wrong.

The Bible is also a love story, a tale of our struggles to find our creator and the victory that will be ours when we do. This struggle began in the Garden of Eden, when Eve first chose to doubt God. We all face this same choice in our lives. The Bible honestly shows the weaknesses of all; even the heroes in this love story are not perfect. All have doubted and most have acted on that doubt. But, God still waits for all of us to come to Him, like a father waiting for his daughter to come home from her first date. The only difference is this Father already knows who will come home to Him. Can you imagine what the father waiting for his daughter to come home would feel, if he already knew she would not return that night? My heart aches at the thought. This is the pain God feels for those who choose to refuse to reason with His Truth.

The Bible is still more; it is an education, an education on life, with answers to every question along the path to truth. Every pain we suffer, every loss we sustain, every love we experience, every friend we find, every truth there is, is explained in the Bible. God did not create us to find our own way in this world, He gave us the Bible to offer us protection from evil and to help us find our way to Him. He wants us to understand He cares about what happens to us, *Jer 29:11, "For I know the thoughts that I think toward you, saith the Lord, thoughts of peace, and not of evil, to give you an expected end."*

The Bible is written in many different writing styles; part allegory, part apocalyptic message, part epistle, part genealogy, part gospel, part history, part the laws that lead to harmony, part parable, part poetry, part prophecy, part song, some symbolism and a wealth of wisdom. Therefore, we cannot take a parable and use it to claim the Bible is not authentic, because a parable cannot be taken literally, for it is a story intended to teach. Context is critical in determining the writing style and the meaning of everything we read in the Bible. The Bible is written in layers, like an onion. The more times we read a verse in context, the more meanings we can gain from it. A verse read today will add new meaning to a verse read a year ago, *Is 28:9-10, "Whom shall he teach knowledge? And whom shall he make to understand doctrine? Them that are weaned from the milk, and drawn from the breasts. For precept must be upon precept, precept upon precept; line upon line, line upon line; here a little, and there a little:"* Those unwilling to study the Bible will never understand it. It will seem like foolishness to them. *Prov 15:14, "The heart of him that hath understanding seeketh knowledge: but the mouth of fools feedeth on foolishness."* This is why we need to read the Bible daily, each day digging deeper into the layers, *Matt 6:11, "Give us this day our daily bread."* The Word of God is our daily bread, *Lk 4:4, "And Jesus answered him, saying, It is written, That man shall not live by bread alone, but by every word of God."*

The better we know the Bible, the more we are able to see the Truth in it. Like any new thing we begin to study in life, the more we learn the more we see we need to learn and how all we have learned begins to come together. We can earn a Ph. D. in life, by studying the Bible, daily. *2 Tim 3:16-17, "All scripture is given by inspiration of God, and is profitable for doctrine, for reproof, for correction, for instruction in righteousness: That the man of God may be perfect, thoroughly furnished unto all good works."*

Peter and John explain one of the more important lessons in understanding the Bible, *Acts 4:19, "But Peter and John answered and said unto them, Whether it be right in the sight of God to hearken unto you more than unto God, judge ye."* Too many in this world have taken the word of Satan over the Word of God. We cannot let ourselves be fooled by Satan's lies and misrepresentations. When we honestly reason with God we can see Satan's lies for what they are. Satan does not love us; he only wants to enslave us. When we watch what people say and do, we learn for ourselves who among us is following God and who is following the lies and misrepresentations of Satan. *Matt 7:16, "Ye shall know them by their fruits. Do men gather grapes of thorns, or figs of thistles?"*

1 Cor 1:20-21, "Where is the wise? where is the scribe? where is the disputer of this world? hath not God made foolish the wisdom of this world? For after that in the wisdom of God the world by wisdom knew not God, it pleased God by the foolishness of preaching to save them that believe." The wisdom of this world has been proven wrong many times, but the good news of the Bible has never been proven wrong. We can accept the foolishness of this world, or we can reason with it. Those who are propagating the foolishness do not want us to reason. They want our unreasoned, uncompromising commitment to their ideology. Does this sound like slavery to their ideas? God does not ask us to blindly accept His Word, He asks us to reason with it before we make mistakes, *Is 1:18, "Come now, and let us reason together, saith the Lord: though your sins be as scarlet, they shall be as white as snow; though they be red like crimson, they shall be as wool."* If after honestly reasoning with God we still want to follow the foolishness, at least it will be a reasoned decision! Why are so many trying to get God out of our lives, out of our schools, off of our money, out of our courts? How does reasoning with God cause us harm? What is the true reason for their actions?

Some think that science has somehow proven the Bible to be inaccurate. When we rightly interpret the Bible and patiently wait for science to catch up, there will be no conflict between the Bible and science. The Bible is the inspired Word of God. Science is the current theory of everything. In the end, science will come to agree with everything the Bible has told us. We know that science has changed its mind many times, but the Bible has never changed one jot or one tittle, *Matt 5:18, "For verily I say unto you, Till heaven and earth pass, one jot or one tittle shall in no wise pass from the law, till all be fulfilled."* God wants us to trust the Bible as His inspired Word, so He placed prophecies into the Bible, so that we might know it is the Truth and that it is from Him. If we need examples of fulfilled Bible Prophecy, we can click this link: Has Bible Prophecy Proven Reliable.[14]

Lk 10:21, "At that time Jesus, full of joy through the Holy Spirit, said, I praise you, Father, Lord of heaven and earth, because you have hidden these things from the wise and learned, and revealed them to little children. Yes, Father, for this is what you were pleased to do." The truth of God's plan is hidden in plain sight. Some of us think we are wise, which makes us too proud to read the Bible with a heart open to learning.

Thus, the Truth is hidden from us. Only when we come to the Bible with the heart of a child willing to learn, can we see the Truth!

Rev 3:20, "Behold, I stand at the door, and knock: if any man hear my voice, and open the door, I will come in to him, and will sup with him, and he with me." The amazing thing is that we have nothing to lose. We can open the door and sup with Him. Once we do, we will see Him for who He is, Lord of Lords, King of Kings, and a loving Father to all who accept His offer. His offer is not for some select few, but rather, He knocks on the door of every person's heart. All are invited!

Here are definitions for the different writing styles used in the Bible, enjoy!

Allegory	A symbolic representation, which can be interpreted to reveal a hidden meaning, typically a moral or political one
Apocalyptic	Message Describing or prophesying the complete destruction of the world
Epistle	A letter
Genealogy	A line of descent traced continuously from an ancestor
Gospel	The teaching or revelation of Christ
History	The study of past events, particularly in human affairs
Law	A system of rules which a particular country or community recognizes and enforces by the imposition of penalties
Parable	A simple story used to illustrate a moral or spiritual lesson, as told by Jesus in the Gospels
Poetry	Literary work in which special intensity is given to the expression of feelings and ideas by the use of distinctive style and rhythm
Prophecy	A prediction of a future event

Songs	A short poem or other sets of words meant to be accompanied by music and/or sung
Symbolism	The use of symbols to represent ideas or qualities
Wisdom	The quality of having experience, knowledge, and good judgment; the quality of being wise.

Can we take the history written in the Bible literally? Recently, I was drawn to watch several videos on the "Old Earth" vs "New Earth" controversy. The following were the two most interesting YouTube videos I watched; one by an Astrophysicist/Cosmologist by the name of Dr. Hugh Ross, and the other by an Applied Scientist/Biologist named Ken Ham. These scientists both believe in God and that the Bible is the inspired Word of God; and both believe there is no conflict between God's inspired Word and science. However, Ken Ham believes we can take the biblical history literally, when God tells us He did something. Here are the links to those two videos: The God Of The Bible Created Everything We See[15] and Ken Ham On Six Days Of Creation.[16]

I am not going to discuss the scientific aspects of the proofs they outline for their belief in the Bible, their knowledge of the subjects make them eminently more qualified to do that. But, I will spend some time on reconciling the only real difference between these two scientists' approach to the Bible.

The age of the earth separates these two scientists approach to explaining creation, as it also separates the teachings of many of today's Christian leaders. Dr. Ross uses stars to verify the truth of the Bible, while Mr. Ham uses scripture alone to point us to the truth of God's Word. If we could somehow reconcile their disagreement on the age of the earth, we could use their combined teachings to bring the truth of the Bible to the light of day and help us better reconcile the perceived difference between science and the Bible.

So, Dr. Ross says that the light coming to us from distant stars proves the old earth concept, because it takes millions or billions of years for light to travel that far. Mr. Ham says that God makes it very clear that it only took Him six days to create everything, *Gen 1:31, "And God saw every thing that he had made, and, behold, it was very good. And the evening and the morning were the sixth day."*

For the believer there is no better source than the Word of the one who created everything, *Job 38:4, "Where wast thou when I laid the foundations of the earth? declare, if thou hast understanding."* But, the skeptic needs to reconcile everything we see in this world to what the Bible claims to be true. We owe it to our creator and ourselves to give the Bible a chance to prove it is the Word of God. Oh, I know about the fossil record and I will get to that before the end of this chapter, but if God created the fossil record He left us the information we need to prove it can be reconciled to His Word. So, let us see if we can use the available information to do just that.

One way to look at the time problem is to consider how long it takes to make something. How many dress shirts can a person make in a day? Seems like a funny question, however, a skilled worker could make two dress shirts in one day. But, an unskilled worker might need a week to finally get one acceptable dress shirt completed. So, the answer to the question is, it depends on who is making the shirt. It will still be a shirt, whether it took four hours or seven days to make. The same principle can be applied to all that God has created. He is capable of creating everything in the blink of an eye, but He tells us He stretched out the process to six days. It is the same finished product, so why did He decide to take six days? He did it to establish a seven-day cycle for us. A cycle that brings us rest every seventh day, a cycle that brings us back to Him and the reasoning with Him that we need. He knows we would drift away without it, *Heb 4:1-4, 8, "Let us therefore fear, lest, a promise being left us of entering into his rest, any of you should seem to come short of it. For unto us was the gospel preached, as well as unto them: but the word preached did not profit them, not being mixed with faith in them that heard it. For we which have believed do enter into rest, as he said, As I have sworn in my wrath, if they shall enter into my rest: although the works were finished from the foundation of the world. For he spake in a certain place of the seventh day on this wise, And God did rest the seventh day from all his works...For if Jesus had given them rest, then would he not afterward have spoken of another day."* Jesus did not come to change anything God had created, including the Sabbath day; He came to confirm what God has told us. *Matt 5:17, "Think not that I am come to destroy the law, or the prophets: I am not come to destroy, but to fulfil."* Science is finally catching up with God on this one. Susan Perry and Jim Dawson report in their book, *The Secrets Our Body Clock Reveal*, that we humans have an internal bodily rhythm of seven days. This cycle does not follow the lunar or solar cycles. For more on this click this link: <u>The Seven Day Human Rhythm.</u>[17] This is just one more opportunity for us to understand that the Bible is from God and that science will eventually agree with the Bible on everything.

Another way to look at the time problem, other than the making of dress shirts, is to think of the last television show we recorded. When we played it back we fast-forwarded through the commercials. Those commercials were still there; we just shortened the time it took to get through them. This is what I believe God did. He created everything in the order He told us He did, and it took Him six days to complete it, however, to us it appears to have taken billions of years. Sort of like someone coming in behind us and watching that same show we recorded without fast-forwarding through the commercials, that person would say it took an hour, when we only spend forty-five minutes. Remember, God told us that we did not create the universe and it did not create itself. God created it and therefore what we are now watching is the fast-forwarded version, which appears to us to have taken billions of years because we were not there to witness the billions of year, however God fast-forwarded through the billions of years in just six days.

The idea being proposed to resolve the conflict between an old earth and a new earth is that it looks like an old earth because God made it that way. He could have slowed the whole creation process down to the billions of years it would have taken. But, He decided to use time as a teaching lesson, a purveyor of the importance of faith. Once we understand that a God big enough to create all that we see is also a God big enough to do it in six days, the apparent conflict dissolves away. Once we leave room for the possibility that God did create in the six days He told us He did, we can begin to honestly evaluate all of the truths of the Bible, most of which have already been proven true, like the seven-day human cycle and the Hayflick discover of our lifetime limit of 120 years! This simple explanation could be the key that unlocks the Bible truths for those who are willing to reason with it.

The main point Ken Ham is making is that when God tells us He did it in six days, we can believe it! It is the devil that keeps asking us to doubt God; "Did God really say He created the earth in six days?" Otherwise, we will not be able to learn the great lessons in the rest of the Bible. Ken Ham uses Bible verses to back up his claim, *Prov 30:5-6, "Every word of God is pure: he is a shield unto them that put their trust in him. Add thou not unto his words, lest he reprove thee, and thou be found a liar."* I would follow that one up with, *Matt 5:18, "For verily I say unto you, Till heaven and earth pass, one jot or one tittle shall in no wise pass from the law, till all be fulfilled."* and *Rev 22:19, "And if any man shall take away from the words of the book of this prophecy, God shall take away his part out of the book of life, and out of the holy city, and from the things which are written in this book."* The Bible is not some book written by fallible humans with an ever-changing truth. The Bible is the infallible Word of God, given to us so that we might find our way to Him, even when the devil tries to lead us through the valley of death! If we will not reason with God we will not obtain the faith we need to understand the truths He has been telling us for thousands of years. *Ps 23:4, "Yea, though I walk through the valley of the shadow of death, I will fear no evil: for thou art with me; thy rod and thy staff they comfort me."*

This is why a true Christian is able to suffer, still be of good spirits and continue to have a positive forward-looking attitude without despair. True Christians know that the devil is working hard to bring us suffering in order to create doubt in our beliefs about God. The devil wants us to believe that a good God would not allow evil. But, the devil is selfish and does not understand someone sacrificing for others, as Jesus did on the cross, or as Paul and Silas did when they were in prison together, *Act 16:25, "And at midnight Paul and Silas prayed, and sang praises unto God: and the prisoners heard them."* Paul and Silas knew that God was with them and that others would benefit from their suffering! *Matt 28:20, "Teaching them to observe all things whatsoever I have commanded you: and, lo, I am with you always, even unto the end of the world. Amen."* It is comforting to know we are not alone and that the time we spend on this earth will be but a very small fraction of the time we will spend in joy with God. *Rom. 8:18, "For I reckon that the sufferings of this present time are not worthy to be compared with the glory which shall be revealed in us."* Our eternal joy will overwhelm the pain and suffering of this present life.

We could discuss how the age of the fossil records are being determined by the decay rates of elements found within the samples. And, we would find that the people doing the dating are presupposing God, whom they do not believe in, is incapable of speeding up the decay rates. Here is a Geologist, Dr. Andrew Snelling discussing the subject: <u>Discussion On Decay Rates</u>.[18] It is a very small God these people do not believe in. My God can do all things, even speed up the decay rate before He creates man. *Matt 19:26, "But Jesus beheld them, and said unto them, With men this is impossible; but with God all things are possible."* After all, He did not want to create humans until He had created all they would need to sustain life and to find their way to Him.

We can talk about how the problems of this world can all be traced back to some defiance of God's laws. He gave us His laws to help us live the longest, happiest, most productive, and joyful lives possible.

We can read the Bible to find His answers to all of our problems. Then we can analyze the results of applying His answers to those problems to determine if they really prove the advice is from God, *2 Tim 3:6-17, "All scripture is given by inspiration of God, and is profitable for doctrine, for reproof, for correction, for instruction in righteousness: That the man of God may be perfect, thoroughly furnished unto all good works."* Notice the Bible says all scripture; we cannot pick and choose the parts we prefer. So, when we are exploring the Bible we must consider the writing style being used and the context of each verse we read. *Is 30:21, "And thine ears shall hear a word behind thee, saying, This is the way, walk ye in it, when ye turn to the right hand, and when ye turn to the left."* To become people of God we have to be willing to listen first, and then we will hear His advice. It is always our choice. *Ps 51:6, "Behold, thou desirest truth in the inward parts: and in the hidden part thou shalt make me to know wisdom."* We all have the Truth hidden in our inward parts, but we will not consciously know it until we are willing to listen. This explains the guilt we feel, even those of us who say we do not believe in God, when we sin, *Lk 16:31, "And he said unto him, If they hear not Moses and the prophets, neither will they be persuaded, though one rose from the dead."* Some of us will not learn, even if we see someone rise from the dead, unless we are first willing to listen with the desire to hear.

1 Pet 1:24-25, "For all flesh is as grass, and all the glory of man as the flower of grass. The grass withereth, and the flower thereof falleth away: But the word of the Lord endureth for ever. And this is the word which by the gospel is preached unto you." Many people and nations have tried to destroy the Bible by either burning all of them, changing it to remove some of God's directions, or forbidding their people from reading it. However, the Bible stands today as the most published book in history and without change. The Dead Sea Scrolls, along with many other ancient documents, have proven the Bible has not changed. It is interesting to note that God chose to hide copies of part of His Bible for thousands of years, so that we could know that it has never changed? What other book in all of history was so preserved? God has left us the evidence, yet so many ignore the evidence and Him. *Matt 24:35, "Heaven and earth shall pass away, but my words shall not pass away."* Even after the heavens and earth are made new we will have the Bible. Click this link to read more on: Proof The Bible Will Never Be Destroyed.[19] The Bible tells us, *Amos 9:14-15, "And I will bring again the captivity of my people of Israel, and they shall build the waste cities, and inhabit them; and they shall plant vineyards, and drink the wine thereof; they shall also make gardens, and eat the fruit of them. And I will plant them upon their land, and they shall no more be pulled up out of their land which I have given them, saith the Lord thy God."* and *Eze 34:13, "And I will bring them out from the people, and gather them from the countries, and will bring them to their own land, and feed them upon the mountains of Israel by the rivers, and in all the inhabited places of the country."* Who would have believed Israel would once again be a nation, after many hundreds of years without one. For more on the fulfilling of this prophecy, click this link: Prophecy Of Israel Becoming A Nation.[20] Yes, the Bible has survived all attempts to destroy it and it will still be around when Jesus returns, and it will be the same Bible we are reading today!

When we follow God's Word, life becomes simple, *Micah 6:8, "He hath shewed thee, O man, what is good; and what doth the Lord require of thee, but to do justly, and to love mercy, and to walk humbly with thy God?"* It is the devil that complicates things, *Gen 3:1, "...And he said unto the woman, Yea, hath God said, Ye shall not eat of every tree of the garden?"* The devil always takes the truth and twists it by either adding or subtracting from it. We, like Eve, follow the distortions because we want what we want. Only when we follow what God truly said are we able to resist the devil, *Matt 16:23, "But he turned, and said unto Peter, Get thee behind me, Satan: thou art an offence unto me: for thou savourest not the things that be of God, but those that be of men."* Jesus wants Peter to understand that the devil is always trying to get us to defy God. God wants us to recognize the devil when we see him and to decide whom we will follow, God or the devil, *Acts 4:19, "But Peter and John answered and said unto them, Whether it be right in the sight of God to hearken unto you more than unto God, judge ye."* And here we come to the heart of the matter, will we follow God, or the lies of the devil. God leads us to peace, rest and joy. This world and the devil's evil lead us to strife, distress and discomfort. When we follow the path away from God, we will never find true peace, rest and joy; no matter how much money, power or fame we have, *Eccl 5:10, "He that loveth silver shall not be satisfied with silver; nor he that loveth abundance with increase: this is also vanity."*

God has described how we are to live in this world, *1 Cor 6:12-13, "All things are lawful unto me, but all things are not expedient: all things are lawful for me, but I will not be brought under the power of any. Meats for the belly, and the belly for meats: but God shall destroy both it and them. Now the body is not for fornication, but for the Lord; and the Lord for the body."* Much of his advice is to help us live a long and healthy life, as opposed to His Ten Commandments, which are not optional. As an example, He tells us not to eat pork. Eating pork will not keep us out of heaven, but not eating it might allow us to live a longer healthier life.

Heb 4:12, "For the word of God is quick, and powerful, and sharper than any twoedged sword, piercing even to the dividing asunder of soul and spirit, and of the joints and marrow, and is a discerner of the thoughts and intents of the heart." God is able to see past what we say and do, to the very thoughts and intents of our hearts! When we go to His Living Word to reason with Him, He knows what we need to hear and gives us just what we need to help us refine our thoughts and move closer to Him. Sometimes it takes years to understand the advice He knows we need, some of us are very slow learners, that is why we need to continue to reason with Him daily. I for one needed to hear some of His messages many times, and in the light of many other verses, before I understood them, and that journey is not over.

Lk 9:23, *"And he said to them all, If any man will come after me, let him deny himself, and take up his cross daily, and follow me."* God is telling us that we need to reason with Him daily and follow the plan He has seen for our lives. Sometimes, He asks us to do things that are uncomfortable. Denying ourselves means we will do what He asks, even when we are uncomfortable doing it.

Rom 1:18, 28-30, *"The wrath of God is being revealed from heaven against all the godlessness and wickedness of people, who suppress the truth by their wickedness...And even as they did not like to retain God in their knowledge, God gave them over to a reprobate mind, to do those things which are not convenient; Being filled with all unrighteousness, fornication, wickedness, covetousness, maliciousness; full of envy, murder, debate, deceit, malignity; whisperers, Backbiters, haters of God, despiteful, proud, boasters, inventors of evil things, disobedient to parents,"* For those who do not believe in God, the truth of these verses is supported by the behavior which is clearly represented on current television under the label of reality shows. Remember, this verse was written nearly two thousand years ago. The wrath of God told to us in this verse, is God getting out of the way and letting our reprobate minds rule our actions.

When we reason with God, we understand the goal He has for us. Once understood, this goal becomes our top priority, *Phil 3:14, "I press on toward the goal to win the prize for which God has called me heavenward in Christ Jesus."*

Heb 12:1, "Wherefore seeing we also are compassed about with so great a cloud of witnesses, let us lay aside every weight, and the sin which doth so easily beset us, and let us run with patience the race that is set before us," God wants us to run the race marked out for us. He wants us to choose to become members of His eternal family. He sets out the race, but it is up to each of us to choose to either run it or ignore it. Ignoring God leaves us alone with "the sin which doth so easily beset us."

When the truths in the Bible are honestly applied they do provide for the best way to live. The Bible is the never changing Word of God.

In the next two chapters we will review God's advice on "How we are to use the Bible" and "How we are to treat others." Maybe, then we will be able to discern their origin, God or man?

How Should We Use The Bible?

If we believe the Bible is the inspired Word of God how should we use it to help us become the people He created us capable of becoming?

The first step begins with our reading and studying, *2 Tim 2:15,* *"Study to shew thyself approved unto God, a workman that needeth not to be ashamed, rightly dividing the word of truth."* We must study the Bible for ourselves. We cannot rely on another person's interpretation, or blindly listen to others, not our friends, not me, and especially not the religious person coming to us in Christ's name. Jesus told us we could not count on others to interpret the Bible for us, *Acts 20:29, "For I know this, that after my departing shall grievous wolves enter in among you, not sparing the flock."* We must reason with God directly, by studying the Bible for ourselves with a will to learn the Truth. Then, we can reason with what all of those other people are telling us. God leads each of us on a personal journey of discovery within His Truth! Each of us will find our own unique personal message from God waiting for us, when we study the Bible for ourselves. God has never changed, yet throughout history people have tried to change the Word of God to fit their needs. This is why we cannot blindly accept their interpretation of His Truth.

In the second step God calls us to use our newly acquired knowledge to help others learn about His Truth! People watch what we do, more than they listen to what we say. If we are to bring them to the Truth, they must first see it in our actions, *2 Cor 4:2, "But have renounced the hidden things of dishonesty, not walking in craftiness, nor handling the word of God deceitfully; but by manifestation of the truth commending ourselves to every man's conscience in the sight of God."* We must be examples, not hypocrites.

Heb 10:23, "Let us hold fast the profession of our faith without wavering; (for he is faithful that promised;)" God's Word will lead us to the person we have been created capable of becoming, but, it will not happen overnight. Each day, each week, and each year we will learn more about God's Truth, as we dig deeper into the layers hidden within His Word. As we dig deeper God sees our faithfulness and gives us more to do, *Matt 25:23, "His lord said unto him, Well done, good and faithful servant; thou hast been faithful over a few things, I will make thee ruler over many things: enter thou into the joy of thy lord."* This is why we cannot ever think we know it all and stop our studies, *Eccl 5:1, "Keep thy foot when thou goest to the house of God, and be more ready to hear, than to give the sacrifice of fools: for they consider not that they do evil."* The person we are when we are first introduced to God will be transformed by our study, if we are willing to hear. Slowly we will become that perfect person God had seen before the beginning of time, *2 Tim 3:16-17, "All scripture is given by inspiration of God, and is profitable for doctrine, for reproof, for correction, for instruction in righteousness: That the man of God may be perfect, thoroughly furnished unto all good works."*

Matt 11:28-30, "Come unto me, all ye that labour and are heavy laden, and I will give you rest. Take my yoke upon you, and learn of me; for I am meek and lowly in heart: and ye shall find rest unto your souls. For my yoke is easy, and my burden is light." When we take up His yoke, we follow His principles for living a godly life. We stop competing with the rest of our brothers and sisters; we work co-operatively with them to produce the best common good. We no longer envy what they have, but rather are happy for them. The feeling of relief we receive from just these two activities lightens our burden and brings rest to our souls. We have become part of a team, rather than the MVP of everything. How does that compare to the "Just Do It" theme that drives this world's winners to use whatever means necessary to win? How can all of those competing to be first ever be happy, how will they ever find rest for their souls?

Luke 4:4, "And Jesus answered him, saying, It is written, That man shall not live by bread alone, but by every word of God." God is telling us that every word He has given us will help us live the life that leads to His eternal family, every word! We will only know the truth of this when we have seen for ourselves how all of His words fit together, when we have worked our way through all of the layers of Truth hidden in His Word. We need to study every word, because if we do not we might miss part of His message to us which is buried in those words we have only given a cursory glance. This requires us to study, daily! This is the message in, *Lk 9:23, "And he said to them all, If any man will come after me, let him deny himself, and take up his cross daily, and follow me."* Denying ourselves means we need to be humble enough to truly reason with God, especially when we think there is disagreement between what we read and what we think we know. We cannot shut God out by not reasoning with Him on these difficult to understand issues. We are not the only losers when we shut God out, for all of those who are counting on our contribution to the common good will also lose.

An example of reasoning with God might help. A friend of mine used the following verse to illustrate that God is somehow unreasonable, *Deut 19:21, "And thine eye shall not pity; but life shall go for life, eye for eye, tooth for tooth, hand for hand, foot for foot."* Let us now reason with God on this subject. *Gen 4:15, "And the Lord said unto him, Therefore whosoever slayeth Cain, vengeance shall be taken on him sevenfold. And the Lord set a mark upon Cain, lest any finding him should kill him."* and *Rom 12:19, "Dearly beloved, avenge not yourselves, but rather give place unto wrath: for it is written, Vengeance is mine; I will repay, saith the Lord."* Clearly these last two verses demonstrate that God does not want us to become vengeful. So, let us go back to the verse in Deuteronomy and put it in context to see the real meaning, *Deut 19:16-21, "If a false witness rise up against any man to testify against him that which is wrong; Then both the men, between whom the controversy is, shall stand before the Lord, before the priests and the judges, which shall be in those days; And the judges shall make diligent inquisition: and, behold, if the witness be a false witness, and hath testified falsely against his brother; Then shall ye do unto him, as he had thought to have done unto his brother: so shalt thou put the evil away from among you. And those which remain shall hear, and fear, and shall henceforth commit no more any such evil among you. And thine eye shall not pity; but life shall go for life, eye for eye, tooth for tooth, hand for hand, foot for foot."* This is not revenge but justice being proposed. It includes a court and judges and establishes a penalty equal to the one the false witness was willing to see carried out on the innocent person. To put it simply, one is law enforcement and the other would be vigilantism. This is why our courts have always had us swear on a Bible before we give our testimony; it is to remind us that we are standing before God. Reasoning with God requires our honest attempts to understand what He is telling us. An interesting side note on this subject is that God always lets us decide our own punishment. Those who choose not to reason with God are deciding their own eternal future. Those who harm innocent people could suffer the consequences of the legal system of the country they are in and will have to deal with their own consciences the rest of their lives.

It is the devil that parses God's words in an attempt to lead us away from God. Remember, the only reason we need laws is that this is not heaven and without laws there are many in this world who would harm us. In heaven we will not need laws, for we will all be righteous, 1 Tim 1:9, *"Knowing this, that the law is not made for a righteous man, but for the lawless and disobedient, for the ungodly and for sinners, for unholy and profane, for murderers of fathers and murderers of mothers, for manslayers,"*

Rom 10:9, "That if thou shalt confess with thy mouth the Lord Jesus, and shalt believe in thine heart that God hath raised him from the dead, thou shalt be saved." Confessing with our mouths is like being baptized, a public demonstration which confirms our unashamed belief and faith in Jesus, *1 Cor 1:17-19, "For Christ sent me not to baptize, but to preach the gospel: not with wisdom of words, lest the cross of Christ should be made of none effect. For the preaching of the cross is to them that perish foolishness; but unto us which are saved it is the power of God. For it is written, I will destroy the wisdom of the wise, and will bring to nothing the understanding of the prudent."* The wisdom of this world will be seen for what it is when Jesus returns, worthless in the face of eternity!

If we do not believe the whole Bible, we might not believe that Jesus rose from the grave, *Lk 16:31, "And he said unto him, If they hear not Moses and the prophets, neither will they be persuaded, though one rose from the dead."* The cross and His resurrection are the indispensible elements of God's message to us. It is the single most important moment in all of human history; the moment God demonstrated the depth of His love for us, His willingness to sacrifice for us! We need to focus on this, instead of the pain and suffering of this evil world.

The third step in how to use the Bible, is applying what we have learned from our reading, praying and reasoning; to develop a clear picture of the life we want to live! One process that leads us to do the will of the Father is called "Life Mapping With Jesus." You can download the book here for free: Life Mapping With Jesus Book.[21]

What is this life about? Why are we here? The answers to these questions can only come from our creator. We cannot trust anyone else to answer them. So, we must look to His Living Word, which He gave us as a manual for this life. *Matt 6:21, "For where your treasure is, there will your heart be also."* The key seems to be the decisions we make regarding those things we treasure in this world and the next.

We will begin with His first four Commandments: *Ex 20:1-11, "And God spake all these words, saying, I am the Lord thy God, which have brought thee out of the land of Egypt, out of the house of bondage. Thou shalt have no other gods before me. Thou shalt not make unto thee any graven image, or any likeness of any thing that is in heaven above, or that is in the earth beneath, or that is in the water under the earth. Thou shalt not bow down thyself to them, nor serve them: for I the Lord thy God am a jealous God, visiting the iniquity of the fathers upon the children unto the third and fourth generation of them that hate me; And shewing mercy unto thousands of them that love me, and keep my commandments. Thou shalt not take the name of the Lord thy God in vain; for the Lord will not hold him guiltless that taketh his name in vain. Remember the sabbath day, to keep it holy. Six days shalt thou labour, and do all thy work: But the seventh day is the sabbath of the Lord thy God: in it thou shalt not do any work, thou, nor thy son, nor thy daughter, thy manservant, nor thy maidservant, nor thy cattle, nor thy stranger that is within thy gates: For in six days the Lord made heaven and earth, the sea, and all that in them is, and rested the seventh day: wherefore the Lord blessed the sabbath day, and hallowed it."* When we put our love for anyone, or anything, before God, our lives become distorted. We work too many hours, worry too much about money, or seek pleasure to the detriment of the truly more important things in our lives. When we put God first and believe He has a plan for us, a plan that is the best one for our lives, everything works out for the best. *Rom 8:28, "And we know that all things work together for good to them that love God, to them who are the called according to his purpose."*

When we put God first, we look past our everyday lives to the vision of God waiting for us at the end of this life. When we put God first we slowly, over a lifetime, change our daily activities to be in alignment with God's plan for us. *Matt 6:33, "But seek ye first the kingdom of God, and his righteousness; and all these things shall be added unto you."* and *Lk 9:62, "And Jesus said unto him, No man, having put his hand to the plough, and looking back, is fit for the kingdom of God."* As we are changing, we cannot look back. The past and all that we have done are just that, the past. We must continue to evolve, becoming the person God created us capable of becoming.

Putting God first allows us to accept that God is the higher power who can lead us out of our addictions and away from evil. It allows us to have a better vision of the person we were created capable of becoming and to work to that end. It allows us to live a more peaceful life, a more thankful life. Putting God first helps us avoid the temptations the devil uses to draw us away from God. Think of the lives destroyed by the addictions of alcohol, drugs, sex, gambling, etc. Most importantly, putting God first helps us shine the light God has given us, so that others might also find their way to God. *Matt 5:16, "Let your light so shine before men, that they may see your good works, and glorify your Father which is in heaven."* Here is a link on: Putting God First.[22]

Why does God warn us not to worship idols and why are we drawn to them? Who do we worship when we worship idols? Ourselves?

I have had my share of idols, the Beatles, the SF Giants, the Warriors, etc. Remembering them sparks a feeling of happiness. When they win, I win. Why am I happy when the Giants win the World Series? Because I picked them, I am on their side in the battle. I am a winner! This is exactly what the devil wants me to think and feel. He ties these feelings to activities that draw me away from God. These feelings are the same ones that the devil uses to draw me into gambling or drinking. I am led to gambling because it provides me with an opportunity to occasionally become that winner, again. I no longer have to wait for the boys of summer to win their way into the World Series; I can gamble and be a winner today! It drives me to drinking because when I am a winner I celebrate it, and when I am a loser, I drown my sorrows. Now, do not get me wrong, I still enjoy the Beatles and watch the Giants and Warriors games. But, I can miss a game, or a song, without it being painful. When the Warriors lost game one in the 2016 playoff series with OKC, I was a little disappointed. Before I understood the proper place for these idols, a loss like that one would have bummed the old me out for days. This time I remembered it was a game and we lost, of no more importance than that. I no longer put these idols ahead of doing what God has called me to do. The devil keeps trying to find those things that will draw me away from doing what God has called me to do. The devil's job gets more difficult each year, as I draw ever closer to God.

Matt 6:24, "No man can serve two masters: for either he will hate the one, and love the other; or else he will hold to the one, and despise the other. Ye cannot serve God and mammon." and *Jn 12:43, "For they loved the praise of men more than the praise of God."* and *Matt 6:21, "For where your treasure is, there will your heart be also."* God is telling us that without Him and His love for us, we will not be able to resist the temptations the devil continually puts before us. The treasures the devil leads us towards will lead us away from God. The solution is to keep God first in our lives.

God has a purpose for all mankind, but He also has a purpose for each of us. When we put idols ahead of God, we cannot fulfill His purpose for our lives. For a deeper look at this problem, see: Worshipping Idols.[23]

The truth that God has a plan for us, for each of us, is a little intimidating at first. We each have the responsibility to work to fulfill that plan. Since, everything God is and does is centered in love, everything we do must also be about others more than ourselves. *Gal 6:1, "Brethren, if a man be overtaken in a fault, ye which are spiritual, restore such an one in the spirit of meekness; considering thyself, lest thou also be tempted. Bear ye one another's burdens, and so fulfil the law of Christ. For if a man think himself to be something, when he is nothing, he deceiveth himself. But let every man prove his own work, and then shall he have rejoicing in himself alone, and not in another. For every man shall bear his own burden. Let him that is taught in the word communicate unto him that teacheth in all good things. Be not deceived; God is not mocked: for whatsoever a man soweth, that shall he also reap."* God wants us to work together to build His church, His eternal family. When any of us distorts the Truth He has given us, we burden those who look to us as examples. We should not be deceived, God knows everything, and we will reap what we sow. This is why God asks each of us to take responsibility for understanding His Word for ourselves. This is why He asks us to reason directly with Him, *Is 1:18, "Come now, and let us reason together, saith the Lord: though your sins be as scarlet, they shall be as white as snow; though they be red like crimson, they shall be as wool."*

When we begin reasoning with God, His Holy Spirit, whom He has placed within each of us, can help us find the path to Him. The Holy Spirit is God working inside us to help us do our part in completing His plan. *Phil 2:13, "For it is God which worketh in you both to will and to do of his good pleasure."* It is the accepting of Jesus as our savior that gives us the faith necessary to fulfill our part in His plan, *Gal 2:20, "I am crucified with Christ: nevertheless I live; yet not I, but Christ liveth in me: and the life which I now live in the flesh I live by the faith of the Son of God, who loved me, and gave himself for me."* He will never reject us, if we are honest about our faith in Him, *Jn 6:37, "All that the Father giveth me shall come to me; and him that cometh to me I will in no wise cast out.*

We no longer have to argue with others or debate whether there is a God. We already know the Truth and will no longer be fooled by old wives' fables or false science trying to prove that there is no

God, 1 Tim 4:7-8, *"But refuse profane and old wives' fables, and exercise thyself rather unto godliness. For bodily exercise profiteth little: but godliness is profitable unto all things, having promise of the life that now is, and of that which is to come."* and 1 Tim 6:20, *"O Timothy, keep that which is committed to thy trust, avoiding profane and vain babblings, and oppositions of science falsely so called:"* Knowing that our generation would become obsessed with false science and physical exercise, to the exclusion of godly pursuits, God is telling us we need to get our priorities straight. He is not saying, we should not learn the truth science could provide, or that we should not exercise. He is saying that these activities come after we have exercised ourselves unto godliness. Sin is anything that separates us from God and the Truth in His Living Word.

Tolerance is required when we begin reasoning with God. As we are transforming into God's vision of ourselves, our ideas of what is right will change. We cannot let these changing ideas puff us up to the detriment of those we are reasoning with. We must reason with others, while listening to their ideas, so that we might grow into God's vision for us, *Rom 14:1-4, "Him that is weak in the faith receive ye, but not to doubtful disputations. For one believeth that he may eat all things: another, who is weak, eateth herbs. Let not him that eateth despise him that eateth not; and let not him which eateth not judge him that eateth: for God hath received him. Who art thou that judgest another man's servant? to his own master he standeth or falleth. Yea, he shall be holden up: for God is able to make him stand."* We are not to judge others. We are to love each other and to share what we have, especially the Word of God. We can reason with each other but each must then decide what they will believe for themselves. No matter where we are on the path to God, others are either ahead or behind us, we must respect the process and allow others to continue to transform without our becoming stumbling blocks for them.

When we put godliness at the top of our priority list, we can be content without a large amount of worldly possessions, *1 Tim 6:7-8,* *"But godliness with contentment is great gain. For we brought nothing into this world, and it is certain we can carry nothing out. And having food and raiment let us be therewith content."* This contentment leads to inner peace and outward harmony. This does not mean we are meant to live in poverty. It means we should not put worldly possessions above godliness. God knows what we need and He wants His children to be happy and healthy. When we follow His guidance we will have both, *Matt 6:33, "But seek ye first the kingdom of God, and his righteousness; and all these things shall be added unto you."*

God created us with a need for rest and recreation. He gave us a day to make sure we do both, the Sabbath, *Mk 2:27, "And he said unto them, The sabbath was made for man, and not man for the sabbath:"* The Sabbath came after He created us, *Eze 20:12, "Moreover also I gave them my sabbaths, to be a sign between me and them, that they might know that I am the Lord that sanctify them."* The Sabbath is all about re-creating our relationships, with God and with other people. As we honor the Sabbath we get closer to God. When we honor the

Sabbath we get closer to those we love. The Sabbath is a sign and time for us to build our relationships.

Understanding the first four Commandments helps us see God more clearly. Hopefully, this will lead us to honestly reason with God. God is in the process of creating the perfect world for His eternal family. This world is not it! He has invited all of us to reason with Him, so that we might come to understand His Truth and choose to spend eternity with Him. He has no other motivation! So, with this in mind, what is keeping us from choosing to be part of His eternal family? What do we lose when we accept His offer? What do we gain by rejecting it? So, how should we use the Bible? The Bible, along with prayer, should be our first sources for answers to all of our questions.

Jn 3:16-17, "For God so loved the world, that he gave his only begotten Son, that whosoever believeth in him should not perish, but have everlasting life. For God sent not his Son into the world to condemn the world; but that the world through him might be saved."

How Should We Treat Each Other?

In an earlier chapter we learned that the Bible is a love letter from God. In His letter, God tells us He loves us, He tells us about the past, present and future; and He also tells us the best way to live. His way of living provides the maximum happiness and joy for the most people, *Ps 16:8-9, 11, "I have set the Lord always before me: because he is at my right hand, I shall not be moved. Therefore my heart is glad, and my glory rejoiceth: my flesh also shall rest in hope...Thou wilt shew me the path of life: in thy presence is fulness of joy; at thy right hand there are pleasures for evermore."* So let us explore some verses to see for ourselves how God asks us to treat each other.

Before we begin, we must understand that this world is not heaven. God's laws and commandments will never be broken in heaven, because everyone there will have seen for themselves that following His way is the best way to live. However, on earth each of us must decide if we will choose to follow Him, *Rom 14:1-4, "Him that is weak in the faith receive ye, but not to doubtful disputations. For one believeth that he may eat all things: another, who is weak, eateth herbs. Let not him that eateth despise him that eateth not; and let not him which eateth not judge him that eateth: for God hath received him. Who art thou that judgest another man's servant? to his own master he standeth or falleth. Yea, he shall be holden up: for God is able to make him stand."* If we choose not to follow God's way, it is because we still do not believe His way is best. So, we must reason with His Word, without

91

arguing, and then we will see the truth of His laws and commandments played out before our eyes in everyday life, as we watch the good and the evil deeds we willingly do. We are only responsible for what we do, so we must not judge others. There are laws in place to judge those who harm others, but we are not judges and we are to show our love to all; thus giving them the freedom to make their own decisions, the same freedom God has given to all of us. Remember, all of this is to create His eternal family who will live for all eternity in love with each other!

His first four commandments are about loving Him, since only those who love Him will be able to follow His way. Everyone else will follow other gods, but there are no other Gods, only false gods created by humans for their own self-interests. We create these false gods to mask our desire for the real God, because we want to live our way, instead of His way. The closer we are to God the harder it is to break any laws, His or the laws of the country we live in, *1 Pet 2:13-15, "Submit yourselves to every ordinance of man for the Lord's sake: whether it be to the king, as supreme; Or unto governors, as unto them that are sent by him for the punishment of evildoers, and for the praise of them that do well. For so is the will of God, that with well doing ye may put to silence the ignorance of foolish men:"* This is how we shine God's love to others, to silence those who prevent others from coming to the real God. The further we are from God the easier it is to break laws, for the only reason we have laws is to protect the innocent from the lawless and disobedient, *1 Tim 1:9-10, "Knowing this, that the law is not made for a righteous man, but for the lawless and* disobedient, for the ungodly and for sinners, for unholy and profane, for murderers of fathers and murderers of mothers, for manslayers, For whoremongers, for them that defile themselves with mankind, for menstealers, for liars, for perjured persons, and if there be any other thing that is contrary to sound doctrine;" So, when we obey the laws, others benefit from our sinless action and can see the fruit of those actions, which will lead more people to God. God is a gentleman and allows us to choose to follow Him or to run from Him. Our choices are the signs others see as they are deciding who they will follow, *Matt 5:13, "Let your light so shine before men, that they may see your good works, and glorify your Father which is in heaven."*

So, let us see what He asks us to do:

God asks us to be selfless, *Gal 2:20, "I am crucified with Christ: nevertheless I live; yet not I, but Christ liveth in me: and the life which I now live in the flesh I live by the faith of the Son of God, who loved me, and gave himself for me."* Giving our lives for others is the ultimate selfless act. Those of us who risk our lives everyday for others, like fireman, soldiers and police officers, demonstrate this selfless behavior, *Phil 2:3, "Let nothing be done through strife or vainglory; but in lowliness of mind let each esteem other better than themselves."* Selfless behavior is humble and does not seek recognition. Compare this humble behavior with this world's need to be recognized and the things people do in that pursuit. There are more award ceremonies today than ever before. I am reminded of two of coach John Wooden's quotes, "Be more concerned with your character than your reputation, because your character is what you really are, while your reputation is merely what others think you are." and "Talent is God given. Be humble. Fame is man-given. Be grateful. Conceit is self-given. Be careful." There is a fine line between fame and conceit and none of us are as good as we pretend to be.

God has asked us to love one another: *1 Jn 4:7-8, "Beloved, let us love one another: for love is of God; and every one that loveth is born of God, and knoweth God. He that loveth not knoweth not God; for God is love."* God can do nothing else, because He is love, *1 Jn 4:16, "And we have known and believed the love that God hath to us. God is love; and he that dwelleth in love dwelleth in God, and God in him."* Love is the common element that unites God's eternal family. *Lev 19:34, "But the stranger that dwelleth with you shall be unto you as one born among you, and thou shalt love him as thyself; for ye were strangers in the land of Egypt: I am the Lord your God."* God wants us to reflect His love onto everyone we meet, so that they might personally feel His love, *Lk 10:27, "And he answering said, Thou shalt love the Lord thy God with all thy heart, and with all thy soul, and with all thy strength, and with all thy mind; and thy neighbour as thyself."* God does not want us to pretend to love Him or our neighbor; He wants us to love our neighbor with all our heart, with all our soul, with all our strength, and with our entire mind. *Lk 11:42, "But woe unto you, Pharisees! for ye tithe mint and rue and all manner of herbs, and pass over judgment and the love of God: these ought ye to have done, and not to leave the other undone."* Pretending did not work for the Pharisees and it will not work for us, *Jn 5:42, "But I know you, that ye have not the love of God in you."* He knows our thoughts. *Jn 3:16, "For God so loved the world, that he gave* his only begotten Son, that whosoever believeth in him should not perish, but have everlasting life." God sent Jesus to help us understand how deeply He loves us. What would this world be like if everyone loved the way God loves?

God asks us to treat our spouses with love: *Gen 2:24, "Therefore shall a man leave his father and his mother, and shall cleave unto his wife: and they shall be one flesh."* The concept of one flesh is compelling, it is difficult to separate something so joined. God wants us to learn to live together in a way that allows our love to grow into His perfect love, always supporting and uplifting one another. *1 Cor 7:3, "Let the husband render unto the wife due benevolence: and likewise also the wife unto the husband."* God wants us to be benevolent to each other, which is defined as well meaning and kind. Everything He teaches us is rooted in love, *Eph 4:31-5:2, "Let all bitterness, and wrath, and anger, and clamour, and evil speaking, be put away from you, with all malice: And be ye kind one to another, tenderhearted, forgiving one another, even as God for Christ's sake hath forgiven you. Be ye therefore followers of God, as dear children; And walk in love, as Christ also hath loved us, and hath given himself for us an offering and a sacrifice to God for a sweetsmelling savour."* If everyone loved their spouses this way, divorce would be a thing of the past. *Matt 19:3-12, "The Pharisees also came unto him, tempting him, and saying unto him, Is it lawful for a man to put away his wife for every cause? And he answered and said unto them, Have ye not read, that he which made them at the beginning made them male and female, And said, For this cause shall a man leave father and mother, and shall cleave to his wife: and they twain shall be one flesh?*

Wherefore they are no more twain, but one flesh. What therefore God hath joined together, let not man put asunder. They say unto him, Why did Moses then command to give a writing of divorcement, and to put her away? He saith unto them, Moses because of the hardness of your hearts suffered you to put away your wives: but from the beginning it was not so. And I say unto you, Whosoever shall put away his wife, except it be for fornication, and shall marry another, committeth adultery: and whoso marrieth her which is put away doth commit adultery. His disciples say unto him, If the case of the man be so with his wife, it is not good to marry. But he said unto them, All men cannot receive this saying, save they to whom it is given. For there are some eunuchs, which were so born from their mother's womb: and there are some eunuchs, which were made eunuchs of men: and there be eunuchs, which have made themselves eunuchs for the kingdom of heaven's sake. He that is able to receive it, let him receive it." God knows that marriage is not the right thing for everyone, each of us must choose for ourselves. However, once chosen, He wants us to put away the strife that destroys marriages and to live together in love. We need to be more thoughtful before we enter into marriage, but when we do, it should be for the rest of our lives. For, if we leave a backdoor to exit by, when we marry, the devil will use it to sneak in and steal our happiness. *Eph 5:33, "Nevertheless let every one of you in particular so love his wife even as himself; and the wife see that she reverence her husband."*

God asks us to teach our children: *Deut 11:18-19, "Therefore shall ye lay up these my words in your heart and in your soul, and bind them for a sign upon your hand, that they may be as frontlets between your eyes. And ye shall teach them your children, speaking of them when thou sittest in thine house, and when thou walkest by the way, when thou liest down, and when thou risest up."* and *Prov 22:6, "Train up a child in the way he should go: and when he is old, he will not depart from it."*

God asks us to honor our parents in His Fifth Commandment, when we are young and when they are old: *Ex 20:12, "Honour thy father and thy mother: that thy days may be long upon the land which the Lord thy God giveth thee."* Here is a link to a discussion on honoring our parents: Honoring Our Parents.[24] Honoring our father and our mother means we respect them and obey them, as long as they act in alignment with God's advice. In the areas that they are in opposition to God, we must follow God, *Acts 5:29, "Then Peter and the other apostles answered and said, We ought to obey God rather than men."* This is why we are to reason with God directly, instead of blindly following a parent, priest, minister, pastor or the devil. This is the mistake the Pharisees made during Jesus' time on earth. Instead of reasoning with Him, they blindly rejected Him, because their motives were not pure. For a deeper Biblical discussion on caring for aging parents, see this link: Caring For Aging Parents.[25]

God asks us to live fearless lives: *Ps 27:1, "The Lord is my light and my salvation; whom shall I fear? the Lord is the strength of my life; of whom shall I be afraid?"* This is why true Christians are not afraid to die, not as suicide terrorists, but as martyrs for Christ Jesus. Christians do not look for death; they accept it as a result of their faith in Christ. Millions of Christians have been killed for their belief in Jesus. Even today thousands die every year, for more on this topic see this link: Christian Martyrs.[26] Compare this lack of fear to those who fear everything in our society, or those that think that God is calling them to kill. God never asks us to kill, on the contrary, He asks us to love our neighbors, to return good for evil, *Lk 6:35, "But love ye your enemies, and do good, and lend, hoping for nothing again; and your reward shall be great, and ye shall be the children of the Highest: for he is kind unto the unthankful and to the evil."* and *Rom 12:21, "Be not overcome of evil, but overcome evil with good."*

God asks us to avoid evil and to call on Him: *Jer 7:8-10, "Behold, ye trust in lying words, that cannot profit. Will ye steal, murder, and commit adultery, and swear falsely, and burn incense unto Baal, and walk after other gods whom ye know not; And come and stand before me in this house, which is called by my name, and say, We are delivered to do all these abominations?"* and *Heb 10:24-25, "And let us consider one another to provoke unto love and to good works: Not forsaking the assembling of ourselves together, as the manner of some is; but exhorting one another: and so much the more, as ye see the day approaching."*

God asks us to shine the light He has given us, so that others might find their way to Him: *1 Pet 3:15, "But sanctify the Lord God in your hearts: and be ready always to give an answer to every man that asketh you a reason of the hope that is in you with meekness and fear:"* When we share the Word of God with non-believers, we are to be meek and gentle, showing them the love of God. *Jam 2:24-26, "Ye see then how that by works a man is justified, and not by faith only. Likewise also was not Rahab the harlot justified by works, when she had received the messengers, and had sent them out another way? For as the body without the spirit is dead, so faith without works is dead also."* Our works are the things we do because we love God and want to follow His way; and this faith helps others see how much we love God and everyone else, including our enemies. Works should be done as a result of faith, without both, we are not saved.

God asks us to forgive others, as we want God to forgive us: *Col 3:12-14, "Put on therefore, as the elect of God, holy and beloved, bowels of mercies, kindness, humbleness of mind, meekness, longsuffering; Forbearing one another, and forgiving one another, if any man have a quarrel against any: even as Christ forgave you, so also do ye. And above all these things put on charity, which is the bond of perfectness."* and *Eph 4:32, "And be ye kind one to another, tenderhearted, forgiving one another, even as God for Christ's sake hath forgiven you."* and *Matt 6:14, "For if ye forgive men their trespasses, your heavenly Father will also forgive you:"*

God asks us to treat everyone the same, no matter their race or position: *Acts 10:28, "And he said unto them, Ye know how that it is an unlawful thing for a man that is a Jew to keep company, or come unto one of another nation; but God hath shewed me that I should not call any man common or unclean."* and *Acts 11:9, "But the voice answered me again from heaven, What God hath cleansed, that call not thou common."* It is not our place to judge which people are cleansed by God. We are to treat everyone equally and give everyone the opportunity to choose to accept Jesus as his or her savior. Those of us who do choose to follow Jesus will one day be in heaven and our old ways will be washed away!

God not only wants us to treat everyone the same, He wants us to work together to encourage each other to good works: *Jam 2:1-13, "My brethren, have not the faith of our Lord Jesus Christ, the Lord of glory, with respect of persons. For if there come unto your assembly a man with a gold ring, in goodly apparel, and there come in also a poor man in vile raiment; And ye have respect to him that weareth the gay clothing, and say unto him, Sit thou here in a good place; and say to the poor, Stand thou there, or sit here under my footstool: Are ye not then partial in yourselves, and are become judges of evil thoughts? Hearken, my beloved brethren, Hath not God chosen the poor of this world rich in faith, and heirs of the kingdom which he hath promised to them that love him? But ye have despised the poor. Do not rich men oppress you, and draw you before the judgment seats? Do not they blaspheme that worthy name by the which ye are called? If ye fulfil the royal law according to the scripture, Thou shalt love thy neighbour as thyself, ye do well: But if ye have respect to persons, ye commit sin, and are convinced of the law as transgressors. For whosoever shall keep the whole law, and yet offend in one point, he is guilty of all. For he that said, Do not commit adultery, said also, Do not kill. Now if thou commit no adultery, yet if thou kill, thou art become a transgressor of the law. So speak ye, and so do, as they that shall be judged by the law of liberty. For he shall have judgment without mercy, that hath shewed no mercy; and mercy rejoiceth against judgment."* God is telling us to follow Him by keeping the whole law, which means we do not pick and choose, which laws we will follow, we follow all of them! *Prov 27:17, "Iron sharpeneth iron; so a man sharpeneth the countenance of his friend."* God asks us to kindly assist each other in developing healthy habits.

God wants us to seek peace whenever possible: *Rom 12:18, "If it be possible, as much as lieth in you, live peaceably with all men."* and *Matt 5:9, "Blessed are the peacemakers: for they shall be called the children of God."* and *Mk 9:50, "Salt is good: but if the salt have lost his saltness, wherewith will ye season it? Have salt in yourselves, and have peace one with another."* and *Lk 1:79, "To give light to them that sit in darkness and in the shadow of death, to guide our feet into the way of peace."* and *Lk 2:13-14, "And suddenly there was with the angel a multitude of the heavenly host praising God, and saying, Glory to God in the highest, and on earth peace, good will toward men."*

God does not want us to offend anyone: *Acts 24:16, "And herein do I exercise myself, to have always a conscience void to offence toward God, and toward men."* and *Matt 18:7, "Woe unto the world because of offences! for it must needs be that offences come; but woe to that man by whom the offence cometh!"* and *1 Cor 10:32, "Give none offence, neither to the Jews, nor to the Gentiles, nor to the church of God:"* God wants us to be kind to everyone! *2 Cor 6:3, "Giving no offence in any thing, that the ministry be not blamed:"* Here we see why we are to offend no one, those offences detract from the ministry of Christ.

God wants us to listen, to learn, to reason, so that we might fulfill our part in His plan for the eternal family: *Jam 1:19, "Wherefore, my beloved brethren, let every man be swift to hear, slow to speak, slow to wrath:"* and *Prov 12:1, "Whoso loveth instruction loveth knowledge: but he that hateth reproof is brutish."* and *Is 1:18, "Come now, and let us reason together, saith the Lord: though your sins be as scarlet, they shall be as white as snow; though they be red like crimson, they shall be as wool."*

God wants us to walk away from sin towards Him and His way: *Jn 8:4, 7, 10-11, "They say unto him, Master, this woman was taken in adultery, in the very act.... So when they continued asking him, he lifted up himself, and said unto them, He that is without sin among you, let him first cast a stone at her... When Jesus had lifted up himself, and saw none but the woman, he said unto her, Woman, where are those thine accusers? hath no man condemned thee? She said, No man, Lord. And Jesus said unto her, Neither do I condemn thee: go, and sin no more."* God does not condemn us in this life, but rather He continues to give us chance after chance to stop our sinning. He is patient and merciful. Contrast this to the unforgiving world we live in, where people will condemn you for the color of your skin, your religion, the country where you were born, the political party you support, etc. I play bridge at a facility surrounded by deserted Fort Ord barracks. About two months ago I drove into the parking lot and saw the following graffiti written on the wall of one of those barracks facing our bridge club, "I hate white people." Yesterday I read that the rioters in Charlotte were chanting, "White people are F_____G devils." People attacking white people are no different than the white people who attack black people. This kind of hatred can be found against all groups, whites, blacks, Christians, Muslims, etc. Fear and hatred are from the devil and will continue to get worse, unless we change the narrative in this country! Check out this link: Discussion on racism.[27] This is not God's way! *Matt 7:3-5, "And why beholdest thou the mote that is in thy brother's eye, but considerest not the beam that is in thine own eye? Or how wilt thou say to thy brother, Let me pull out the mote out of thine eye; and, behold, a beam is in thine own eye? Thou hypocrite, first cast out the beam out of thine own eye; and then shalt thou see clearly to cast out the mote out of thy brother's eye."* We must first remove the sin in our own lives, before we can help others see how evil sin is.

God wants us to seek righteousness and eschew evil: *1 Pet 3:8-12, "Finally, be ye all of one mind, having compassion one of another, love as brethren, be pitiful, be courteous: Not rendering evil for evil, or railing for railing: but contrariwise blessing; knowing that ye are thereunto called, that ye should inherit a blessing. For he that will love life, and see good days, let him refrain his tongue from evil, and his lips that they speak no guile: Let him eschew evil, and do good; let him seek peace, and ensue it. For the eyes of the Lord are over the righteous, and his ears are open unto their prayers: but the face of the Lord is against them that do evil."* and *Matt 6:33, "But seek ye first the kingdom of God, and his righteousness; and all these things shall be added unto you."* We are not to put our wants before God's desire for us to seek righteousness. The cool thing is that He will take care of our wants when we do. *Rom 12:9, "Let love be without dissimulation. Abhor that which is evil; cleave to that which is good."* Dissimulation is the very antithesis of honesty. There are too many hypocrites in our society and few are challenging them. We must each look for the hypocrisies in our own lives and cling to the good, instead.

God wants us to follow the laws of the land we live in: *1 Pet 2:13-15, "Submit yourselves to every ordinance of man for the Lord's sake: whether it be to the king, as supreme; Or unto governors, as unto them that are sent by him for the punishment of evildoers, and for the praise of them that do well. For so is the will of God, that with well doing ye may put to silence the ignorance of foolish men:"* God is using our obedience to show the world His light! We are not to pick and choose which laws we will obey. God wants us to obey all of the laws, because He wants to silence His critics. What would this world be like if everyone obeyed all of the laws? As Abraham Lincoln once said, "The best way to get a bad law repealed is to enforce it strictly." If we all followed all of the laws, the bad ones would become irrelevant.

God asks us to avoid killing: God feels so strongly about killing that He directed us in His Ten Commandments not to kill. What would this world be like without killing? *Ex 20:13, "Thou shalt not kill."* and *Deut 5:17, "Thou shalt not kill."* and *Gen 4:15, "And the Lord said unto him, Therefore whosoever slayeth Cain, vengeance shall be taken on him sevenfold. And the Lord set a mark upon Cain, lest any finding him should kill him."* God began warning us not to seek vengeance from the very first murder in history. *Prov 6:16-19, "These six things doth the Lord hate: yea, seven are an abomination unto him: A proud look, a lying tongue, and hands that shed innocent blood, An heart that deviseth wicked imaginations, feet that be swift in running to mischief, A false witness that speaketh lies, and he that soweth discord among brethren."* God gives us a pretty short list of the things He hates, but the shedding of innocent blood is one of them. Where is there room for terrorism in this statement from God? No one can honestly commit acts of terrorism in the name of God. Those who do commit these acts are misinformed, dishonest or truly willing to do evil works.

God does not want us to steal: *Ex 20:15, "Thou shalt not steal."* Stealing destroys peace, trust and relationships. Stealing is a product of self-love and when we take God out of our lives, it is easy to rationalize stealing. Here is a link to Quora where some atheists discuss stealing: <u>Atheists Views On Stealing</u>.[28] Atheists rationalize the judgment on stealing as something that depends on the given situation. God tells us that stealing is always wrong and separates us from Him and His love. We can never rationalize stealing. When we refuse to allow stealing to be an option, God will provide a way for us, *Rom 8:28, "And we know that all things work together for good to them that love God, to them who are the called according to his purpose."* When we choose to put ourselves first, the devil moves in and we suffer the consequences of a life without a relationship with God. The devil does not love us and only provides for us until he is able to addict us into slavery. Then, he treats us like the slaves we have become and uses us to enslave others, *Matt 13:38-40, "The field is the world; the good seed are the children of the kingdom; but the tares are the children of the wicked one; The enemy that sowed them is the devil; the harvest is the end of the world; and the reapers are the angels. As therefore the tares are gathered and burned in the fire; so shall it be in the end of this world."* Does it sound like the tares, which are sowed by the devil, are anything but slaves? This does not paint a very pretty ending for our making the wrong choice, but as we have learned, God cannot lie! *Tit 1:2, "In hope of eternal life, which God, that cannot lie, promised before the world began;"*

God does not want us to bare false witness: *Ex 20:16, "Thou shalt not bear false witness against thy neighbour."* This covers so many areas in our conversational lives; falsely testifying at a trial, lying, gossiping, breaking confidences, the horrors of spreading vial speech in social media, etc. *1 Pet 2:17, "Honour all men. Love the brotherhood. Fear God. Honour the king."*

God has told us that He cannot lie, *Tit 1:2, "In hope of eternal life, which God, that cannot lie, promised before the world began;"* But, why is telling the truth so important to God? Because He wants us to know that every promise He makes, He keeps. He wants us to do the same, so that our light might shine bright enough to attract others to His Living Word. Lying can open the door to unintended consequences, as this link demonstrates: The Consequences Of Lying.[29] Lying is the work of the devil and those who continue in it are his slaves, *Jn 8:44, "Ye are of your father the devil, and the lusts of your father ye will do. He was a murderer from the beginning, and abode not in the truth, because there is no truth in him. When he speaketh a lie, he speaketh of his own: for he is a liar, and the father of it."* The devil is so paranoid that his slaves might lie to him that he is willing to kill them if he even suspects they might be lying to him. One of the major results of lying is that eventually we can no longer trust others, since we come to believe everyone is a liar. Here is a link to a modern day example of this principle at work: Lack Of Trust

Leading To Killing.[30] Faith is the fruit of God and distrust is the fruit of the devil. Another great example of loss of trust is our current group of politicians; so many of them are willing to lie, that we as a society have come to believe that all of them are liars.

God does not want us to envy what other people have: In His Tenth Commandment God tells us we should not envy anything or anyone, *Ex 20:17*, *"Thou shalt not covet thy neighbour's house, thou shalt not covet thy neighbour's wife, nor his manservant, nor his maidservant, nor his ox, nor his ass, nor any thing that is thy neighbour's"*: What does envy lead to? Envy might lead us to steal, or it might cause us to be dissatisfied with our lives. For many of us this dissatisfaction becomes so severe we are unable to see a way out, and this feeling of hopelessness has led many of us to see suicide as an option, as seen in this link: Suicide In The US.[31] Reasoning with God tells us we have hope and that this world is not the end, if we choose God. This hope helps us take the suicide option off the table, *Rom 12:12, 21*, *"Rejoicing in hope; patient in tribulation; continuing instant in prayer; Be not overcome of evil, but overcome evil with good."* When we have hope we go to God in prayer and work to overcome the evil of this world with good; we are able to overcome our dissatisfaction with this life, we look to God to lead us to help others deal with the evil of this world. Our focus shifts from ourselves to others. The tribulations we face dim in the light of our godly service to others. Remember, God will comfort us in our tribulations, so that we might comfort others, *2 Cor 1:3-4*, *"Blessed be God, even the Father of our Lord Jesus Christ, the Father of mercies, and the God of all comfort;*

Who comforteth us in all our tribulation, that we may be able to comfort them which are in any trouble, by the comfort wherewith we ourselves are comforted of God." Years ago we taught our children about God and they learned to have His hope, faith in a higher power. Our belief in God will help us deal with our current suicide problem. When we help others, we are no longer left alone in our tribulations.

God wants us to give to those in need: *Lk 6:38, "Give, and it shall be given unto you; good measure, pressed down, and shaken together, and running over, shall men give into your bosom. For with the same measure that ye mete withal it shall be measured to you again."* and *Rom 15:1-2, "We then that are strong ought to bear the infirmities of the weak, and not to please ourselves. Let every one of us please his neighbour for his good to edification."* We are to give money, time, compassion and understanding, to name a few.

God wants us to care for the bodies He has given us: A version of God's recommended diet has helped the Seventh Day Adventists live longer lives, *Gen 1:29-30, "And God said, Behold, I have given you every herb bearing seed, which is upon the face of all the earth, and every tree, in the which is the fruit of a tree yielding seed; to you it shall be for meat. And to every beast of the earth, and to every fowl of the air, and to every thing that creepeth upon the earth, wherein there is life, I have given every green herb for meat: and it was so."* God started us with a vegan diet. Everyone's diet changed after the flood. *Gen 9:3-4, "Every moving thing that liveth shall be meat for you; even as the green herb have I given you all things. But flesh with the life thereof, which is the blood thereof, shall ye not eat."* This change in diet was required, since all of the earth had been under water and the earth had to replenish itself before we could eat grains and fruits, again.

Eze 4:9, "Take thou also unto thee wheat, and barley, and beans, and lentiles, and millet, and fitches, and put them in one vessel, and make thee bread thereof, according to the number of the days that thou shalt lie upon thy side, three hundred and ninety days shalt thou eat thereof." God is telling us, through Ezekiel, that this diet is all we need to survive and thrive. God was preparing Israel for war. He was also telling us that luxurious eating is not necessary to sustain life. The luxurious lifestyles we live today usually include excessive eating and drinking, which are not healthy. God wants us to understand that there is a cost to be paid for all of our choices. He is not forcing us to eat His recommended diet; He just wants us to know we might face health problems as the result of ignoring it, *Dan 1:11-12, "Then said Daniel to Melzar, whom the prince of the eunuchs had set over Daniel, Hananiah, Mishael, and Azariah, Prove thy servants, I beseech thee, ten days; and let them give us pulse to eat, and water to drink."* God makes it clear in Daniel that a vegan diet with water to drink is still the healthiest one. It is the diet that allows us to function at our best. *2 Sam 17:28-29, "Brought beds, and basons, and earthen vessels, and wheat, and barley, and flour, and parched corn, and beans, and lentiles, and parched pulse, And honey, and butter, and sheep, and cheese of kine, for David, and for the people that were with him, to eat: for they said, The people is hungry, and weary, and thirsty, in the wilderness."* Another example of the diet God has given us to eat. *Phil 4:5, "Let your moderation be known unto all men. The Lord is at hand."* Knowing that most humans would not stick to a strictly vegan or vegetarian diet, once they had tasted meats, God advises us to limit the amount of everything we eat and drink. It is this moderation that allows humans to avoid most of the problems that excesses bring. *Prov 25:27-28, "It is not good to eat much honey: so for men to search their own glory is not glory. He that hath no rule over his own spirit is like a city that is broken down, and without walls."* This world has changed the idea of a good diet many times over the years and is now moving closer to the diet God has been telling us is best for thousands of years. What would this world be like if everyone followed God's recommended diet? For more info on Biblical Advice on diet, click: Biblical Advice On Diet[32] and Biblical Foods By Verse.[33]

1 Cor 6:19-20, "What? know ye not that your body is the temple of the Holy Ghost which is in you, which ye have of God, and ye are not your own? For ye are bought with a price: therefore glorify God in your body, and in your spirit, which are God's." and *Prov 19:15, "Slothfulness casteth into a deep sleep; and an idle soul shall suffer hunger."* and *Eccl 10:18, "By much slothfulness the building decayeth; and through idleness of the hands the house droppeth through."* God created us with bodies so that we might do the work He has assigned to us. Our bodies are not made to be idle. Our bodies need the exercise that comes from honest work to stay healthy. When we ignore the needs of the body, through slothfulness or misuse, we destroy the body and are no longer able to complete the work assigned to us. God's light is no longer able to shine as brightly and thus we draw fewer people to God and His eternal salvation.

Gen 2:2-3, "And on the seventh day God ended his work which he had made; and he rested on the seventh day from all his work which he had made. And God blessed the seventh day, and sanctified it: because that in it he had rested from all his work which God created and made." Surely, God did not need to rest; He rested as an example for all of us. *Mk 2:27, "And he said unto them, The sabbath was made for man, and not man for the sabbath:"* God wants us to know that He made a Sabbath day for us, because we need to take breaks from our work. *Matt 12:8, "For the Son of man is Lord even of the sabbath day."* God wants us to know that Jesus is the Lord of the Sabbath day and that this is the day we are to rest. *Matt 11:28, "Come unto me, all ye that labour and are heavy laden, and I will give you rest."* When we follow God's plan we will see the benefits of the rest He has given us. Science is finally catching up with God's plan, as demonstrated by a series of discoveries during the period of 1965 to 1990 that the human body has a seven-day cycle, here is the link: <u>Circaseptan Rhythm In Humans</u>.[34] *Ps 127:2, "It is vain for you to rise up early, to sit up late, to eat the bread of sorrows: for so he giveth his beloved sleep."* God wants us to know that we need a good nights sleep to be at our best, His beloved sleep. Science discovered that we also have a twenty-four hour cycle, which requires us to sleep each night, here is the link: <u>Circadian Rhythm In Humans</u>.[35] These periods of rest allow our bodies and our minds to store the information we have acquired each day, the time we need to replenish our energy and to reset our internal mechanisms, which allows us to function at the level God created us capable of performing. It is interesting to note that people think highly of science, without recognizing that God told us these things thousands of years before science discovered them.

God gives us a lifetime to reason with His Living Word, to refine our thoughts and to judge for ourselves the value of His advice. We now see God's advice with our own eyes. What part of His advice is evil, or arduous? Does this mean that those who speak against God are against His advice? *Jam 2:10, "For whosoever shall keep the whole law, and yet offend in one point, he is guilty of all."* When we accept Jesus as our savior, we consciously work to keep the whole law. We no longer make up excuses to justify breaking any of them. When we do break one of them, we seek forgiveness and repent from repeating the error. True remorse should be the tenor of our apologies. We cannot pretend, God knows everything we do, every word we speak and every thought we think. Nothing is hidden from God, *Ps 44:21, "Shall not God search this out? for he knoweth the secrets of the heart."*

Rom 7:12, "Wherefore the law is holy, and the commandment holy, and just, and good." God gives us His advice to make our lives better. But, many think His laws and commandments are meant to somehow restrict us. I believe God's advice is good and does lead us to the best and happiest life in this world and the next. Why do I believe this? Because I have lived long enough to see what evil does to people and it is not pretty.

We have heard God's advice and it is good!

1 Jn 5:3, "For this is the love of God, that we keep his commandments: and his commandments are not grievous." God tells us that the keeping

His laws and commandments is not grievous; in fact, they are meant to help lead us to Him and His peace in this life and to the eternal future He promises.

Why do so many ignore God and His Bible?

What Is God's Plan?

"One God, one law, one element, And one far-off divine event, To which the whole creation moves." — Alfred Lord Tennyson

God chose love and free-will to be at the heart of His plan, *Deut 30:19, "I call heaven and earth to record this day against you, that I have set before you life and death, blessing and cursing: therefore choose life, that both thou and thy seed may live:"* He wants each of us to learn who He is, what He is like and to use this information to choose whether we want to live with Him for all eternity, or not, *Prov 2:1-2, 5, "My son, if thou wilt receive my words, and hide my commandments with thee; So that thou incline thine ear unto wisdom, and apply thine heart to understanding;...Then shalt thou understand the fear of the Lord, and find the knowledge of God."* He knows that this will lead to our loving Him, *1 Jn 4:7-8, "Beloved, let us love one another: for love is of God; and every one that loveth is born of God, and knoweth God. He that loveth not knoweth not God; for God is love."*

God loves us so much that He wants each of us to feel the love of everyone else in His eternal family. If I decided to throw the greatest party in history and sent an invitation to every living person, but asked only those who truly love me to come, what would happen? People would begin lining up to come to the greatest party of all time, the vast majority would not even know who I am, much less love me. I would not know for sure who really loves me. But, I am not the one with two scarred hands. When He invites everyone to His party, He already knows who will choose to reason with Him, which will lead them to love Him. Since, they love Him, they will also love everyone else at the party. Now, that is a real party, not some fake Hollywood party where people go to be seen. There will be no one pretending to love us at God's party. The pretenders will not be allowed in.

This is why His plan requires each of us to choose for ourselves; we either reason with God to learn the Truth or refuse to even reason with Him. It is the reasoning with God that teaches us His nature, His very being, which is love. Those who choose to reason with God will not only learn about love, they will also learn to love themselves, love God and love everyone else. His eternal family will be knit together in love, *Col 2:2, "That their hearts might be comforted, being knit together in love, and unto all riches of the full assurance of understanding, to the acknowledgement of the mystery of God, and of the Father, and of Christ;"* and *1 Jn 4:20, "If a man say, I love God, and hateth his brother, he is a liar: for he that loveth not his brother whom he hath seen, how can he love God whom he hath not seen?"* The people at God's party will not only love each other, they will love those who chose not to come. Those who chose not to come will not even love each other, much less all of those at the party. God can see through our masks to the people we really are and what we really believe. We cannot pretend and fool God. We cannot hide our true feelings from God. *Gen 3:9, "And the Lord God called unto Adam, and said unto him, Where art thou?"* We might hear God asking where we are, but rest assured, He already knows where we are. The solution is to reason with Him and then make our final decision.

We are born, some into an environment that promotes the study of God's Word, and some into an environment that ridicules or condemns God and/or the study of His Word.

Those fortunate enough to have easy access to the Bible will be challenged to accept someone else's interpretation rather than study it for themselves. *Jer 12:10, "Many pastors have destroyed my vineyard, they have trodden my portion under foot, they have made my pleasant portion a desolate wilderness."* The devil uses the seemingly similar deception of a false religion to draw those of us most likely to seek the path to God, away from the Truth. This is probably the devil's last chance to stop us from accepting Jesus as our savior. God wants each of us to reason with Him, directly! So, we who have been fortunate enough to have the Bible at our fingertips must read it for ourselves! We cannot take anyone else's interpretation, not mine, not our pastor's, not our best friends, we must learn for ourselves! When we come to the Day of Judgment we will not be able to blame someone else, for our own unwillingness will testify against us.

Those who start this life under the veil of hatred and loathing for God can still find the seed of God's love by observing the hatred and cruelty being demonstrated under the guise of another religion or atheism, *Rom 5:5-6, "And hope maketh not ashamed; because the love of God is shed abroad in our hearts by the Holy Ghost which is given unto us. For when we were yet without strength, in due time Christ died for the ungodly."* God is telling us that the Holy Ghost is spreading the love of God to all people. Jesus died for all of us before we were with strength, which means before we even knew He existed. Remember, even the disciples, those closest to Him did not understand what was happening when He was being crucified. Those who are under the veil of hatred will feel the Holy Ghost moving them. If they accept this feeling, it will help them see the evil they are living with and eventually, they will be led to accept the love of God. It will be a choice. Even though these people do not understand what is happening, they are fighting for their religious freedom. Fighting for the right to freely choose to worship the God they believe in, without being persecuted, *Is 33:15, "He that walketh righteously, and speaketh uprightly; he that despiseth the gain of oppressions, that shaketh his hands from holding of bribes, that stoppeth his ears from hearing of blood, and shutteth his eyes from seeing evil;"* When the love of God is accepted, evil will be seen for what it is and despised. When this happens, people will be open to the Word of God and God will bring it to them. This will lead to reasoning with God. This is why He is busy sending His messengers to every part of the world, with the Bible translated into every language, *Rev 14:6, "And I saw another angel fly in the midst of heaven, having the everlasting gospel to preach unto them that dwell on the earth, and to every nation, and kindred, and tongue, and people,"* We need to look around, God is doing His part, are we paying attention? *Jer 5:21, "Hear now this, O foolish people, and without understanding; which have eyes, and see not; which have ears, and hear not:"* He has been telling us about this problem for thousands of years. Why are we still ignoring Him?

Once we choose to reason with God, we will be challenged at every turn. Some will challenge our belief, some will try to prove other religions are equally valid, some will make fun of our newly found interest in religion, and some will try to harm us in an effort to silence us. *Ex23:20, "Behold, I send an Angel before thee, to keep thee in the way, and to bring thee into the place which I have prepared."* He is telling us we have an angel to help keep us in the way, but we have the choice of hearing what that angel is saying or rejecting that help. Dealing with the challenges the devil will bring will be much easier if we are willing to reason with God to hear about "the way" He has prepared for us.

Rom 5:3-4, "And not only so, but we glory in tribulations also: knowing that tribulation worketh patience; And patience, experience; and experience, hope:" The tribulations we face in this life drive some of us to seek answers. Those answers lead some of us to God and His peace. Once we experience reasoning with God, we are further rewarded with the hope of the promise He offers of an eternal life. God could prevent us from experiencing these tribulations, however, He knows some of us need this experience to find our way to Him. Just as He knew Jesus would have to come, suffer horrible pain and be crucified for us. He is not creating these tribulations; they are a result of the interference of the devil; the same interference Job experienced and the same interference that has given us the rebellious nature we inherited from Adam and Eve.

Josh 24:15, "And if it seem evil unto you to serve the Lord, choose you this day whom ye will serve; whether the gods which your fathers served that were on the other side of the flood, or the gods of the Amorites, in whose land ye dwell: but as for me and my house, we will serve the Lord." Joshua might have needed those forty years of wandering in the desert, personally witnessing God at work, to fully accept God and His plan for Joshua and his entire family. Those forty years of tribulations might have led Joshua to choose God!

Ps 25:12, "What man is he that feareth the Lord? him shall he teach in the way that he shall choose." The meaning of the word "feareth" being used in this verse is "in awe of." When we truly understand who God is, what He has already done, and what He is capable of doing, we are awestruck. When we are in this state, it is easy for God to get His Truth to us.

Prov 1:31-33, "Therefore shall they eat of the fruit of their own way, and be filled with their own devices. For the turning away of the simple shall slay them, and the prosperity of fools shall destroy them. But whoso hearkeneth unto me shall dwell safely, and shall be quiet from fear of evil." God loves us so much He is willing to let us walk away from Him, even to our own death, *Eze 33:11, "Say unto them, As I live, saith the Lord God, I have no pleasure in the death of the wicked; but that the wicked turn from his way and live: turn ye, turn ye from your evil ways; for why will ye die, O house of Israel?"* CS Lewis poses a good question, "Should God save people against their will?" The answer is no, because He is love and love requires free will. So, He keeps calling us, to assure He has given us every possible chance to reason with the Truth He is freely offering, 2 *Pet 3:9, "The Lord is not slack concerning his promise, as some men count slackness; but is longsuffering to us-ward, not willing that any should perish, but that all should come to repentance."* He wants all of us to listen and learn, however, He knows many will not. God created us to feel the same things He feels. This is why His plan includes families for us. We can thus imagine how God feels when we walk away, by imagining how we would feel if our children decided to walk away from us and do something we know will cause them pain and suffering; while all we can do is watch as they reap the results of their choices.

Rev 21:6–7, "And he said unto me, It is done. I am Alpha and Omega, the beginning and the end. I will give unto him that is athirst of the fountain of the water of life freely. He that overcometh shall inherit all things; and I will be his God, and he shall be my son." and *Rom 6:23, "For the wages of sin is death; but the gift of God is eternal life through Jesus Christ our Lord."* Our choice.

Grace plays a big part in His plan. So, what is grace? Grace is God's loving offer of salvation to the undeserved rebellious people He created.

"Grace is love that cares and stoops and rescues." - John Stott.

"Grace is the opposite of karma, which is all about getting what you deserve. Grace is getting what you do not deserve, and not getting what you do deserve." - From Christianity.com

Titus 2:11-14, "For the grace of God that bringeth salvation hath appeared to all men, Teaching us that, denying ungodliness and worldly lusts, we should live soberly, righteously, and godly, in this present world;

Looking for that blessed hope, and the glorious appearing of the great God and our Saviour Jesus Christ; Who gave himself for us, that he might redeem us from all iniquity, and purify unto himself a peculiar people, zealous of good works." Titus shows us that salvation has appeared to all men, however, we must not be fooled into thinking that God will allow evil to exist in the next world. God transforms us by bringing us through a purification process, so that He will have a peculiar people in Heaven, and they will be zealous of good works, those unwilling to do good works will not be in Heaven. Zechariah wants us to understand this transformation process, *Zech 13:9, "And I will bring the third part through the fire, and will refine them as silver is refined, and will try them as gold is tried: they shall call on my name, and I will hear them: I will say, It is my people: and they shall say, The Lord is my God."* Zealous means we are eager to learn what good works are. We are willing to live intentionally in an effort to adopt God's good works, to examine our lives, and to humble ourselves enough to learn the lessons God makes so clear to those who have a desire to learn them.

Eph 1:4-5, "According as He hath chosen us in Him before the foundation of the world, that we should be holy and without blame before Him in love: Having predestinated us unto the adoption of children by Jesus Christ to Himself, according to the good pleasure of His will," Paul makes it clear that before God created us, He looked into the future, saw those who would accept His grace and His adoption as children by Jesus Christ. So, there are two parts to grace, God offers it and we accept it, and not everyone will choose to accept His offer.

So, grace was in the past, is in the present and will be in the future! We are all in the process of understanding it, accepting it and then being transformed by it, or not.

2 Tim 3:16-17, "All scripture is given by inspiration of God, and is profitable for doctrine, for reproof, for correction, for instruction in righteousness: That the man of God may be perfect, thoroughly furnished unto all good works." This is why the proud run from His Word. The proud have no desire to learn lessons, they want to be free to live anyway they want. They are obsessed with what this world believes makes us happy. Their vision is on the present and they are lured by immediate gratifications. Those who make it through the fire will have their vision set on eternity and God's Heavenly family. Those who choose to accept grace will no longer be lured into evil acts, they will no longer be willing to sit back and ignore the evil acts others are doing, for they will have learned what good works are and will have fixed their eyes on Heaven.

The great thing about grace is that it is offered to everyone! Why does this offer go out to everyone, instead of only those who do good works? Because, God loves all of us and we have all sinned. God is fair, allowing for everyone to have the opportunity to believe, to accept His forgiveness and to repent. He knows only humble people will be willing to admit they have sinned, *Rom 3:23, "For all have sinned, and come short of the glory of God;"* It is not our sins that will keep us from an eternity with God, it is our stubbornness, our unwillingness to accept His forgiveness, to admit our sins and to repent from them.

An example might help with this concept; a man, talking on his cell phone, is getting in line to buy some tickets when he notices that he inadvertently cut in front of a woman who was already in line. He now tells her he is sorry, asks her to excuse his bad behavior and finally directs her to move ahead of him to her proper place in line. He could have pretended he had not noticed she was there and continued to leave her behind him. He could have said he was sorry, not asked for her forgiveness and still left her behind. He could have said he was sorry, asked for her forgiveness and still left her behind. Saying he was sorry was the recognition he had done something wrong. His asking for her forgiveness shows that he truly is sorry, a form of confessing his sin, not just giving her a line to justify his bad behavior, 1 Jn 1:9, "If we confess our sins, he is faithful and just to forgive us our sins, and to cleanse us from all unrighteousness." The act of moving behind her is an act of repentance and increases the odds that he will not repeat this bad behavior. He is learning and will be a little more careful the next time. God's purification process requires all three, for that is the only way we will be humble enough to treat people in Heaven with the love God has shown to all of us. It begins with faith and is completed by works, Eph 2:8-10, "For by grace are ye saved through faith; and that not of yourselves: it is the gift of God: Not of works, lest any man should boast. For we are his workmanship, created in Christ Jesus unto good works, which God hath before ordained that we should walk in them." This is why we feel good when we do good things. This is also why we feel guilty when we do evil things. The reason we feel these things is God created us with a moral compass, a conscience. When we do evil things our guilt either drives us back towards God, or further away from Him, as we try to prove we really are the evil people we now think we are. God wants us to choose to repent and follow Him, as our response to our feelings of guilt. God knows that our evil deeds alone do not make us evil people, it is only when we have completely turned our back on God, and our required repentance, that we become slaves to the evil one.

God's gift to us is grace, but we must accept it. Just as someone sending a gift to another person, it must be accepted for that gift to actually be enjoyed. If the receiver refuses the delivery, the gift is lost to them. God's grace is offered to all, however, only those willing to humble themselves will be refined as silver and fit to be called His people. This is a choice we must each make for ourselves. When we do, we move ever closer to God and our increasingly good works testify to the fact we are saved. Good works do not save us; they are only the proof we are saved. We cannot be saved without faith, which leads to good works, *Jam 2:14, 17, "What doth it profit, my brethren, though a man say he hath faith, and have not works? can faith save him?... Even so faith, if it hath not works, is dead, being alone."* Only when we truly believe do we act on that belief in the form of good works.

Grace is necessary because we have all sinned. There is evil in this world and this evil attempts to lure us further down the road leading away from God, *2 Pet 2:18-19, "For when they speak great swelling words of vanity, they allure through the lusts of the flesh, through much wantonness, those that were clean escaped from them who live in error. While they promise them liberty, they themselves are the servants of corruption: for of whom a man is overcome, of the same is he brought in bondage."* Grace frees us from the evil way, makes the way of Truth known to us and transforms our desires, motivations, and behavior, 2 Pet 2:9, *"The Lord knoweth how to deliver the godly out of temptations, and to reserve the unjust unto the day of judgment to be punished:"* God created a way for us to find the path to His eternal family. It is not hidden, except from those too proud to look for it.

The fact that Jesus has not yet returned has led some to believe that He will not return, 2 Pet 3:9, *"The Lord is not slack concerning his promise, as some men count slackness; but is longsuffering to us-ward, not willing that any should perish, but that all should come to repentance."* The proud use this seeming delay as their excuse to live a life separated from God. What will they say to God on the day they face Him, alone, for judgment? It will be a daunting moment; but fear not, for He has prepared a way for us, Grace, *Rev 20:12*, *"And I saw the dead, small and great, stand before God; and the books were opened: and another book was opened, which is the book of life: and the dead were judged out of those things which were written in the books, according to their works."* A benevolent God draws us; all we have to do is recognize His benevolence!

John tells us that no matter what sin we have committed, Jesus is willing to be our advocate at the judgment seat, 1 Jn 2:1, *"My little children, these things write I unto you, that ye sin not. And if any man sin, we have an advocate with the Father, Jesus Christ the righteous:"*

When we understand this, we can allow the transformation process to begin, *Phil 4:13, "I can do all things through Christ which strengtheneth me."* When we accept God's grace we can call on Jesus to help us do all things, as we work to complete the transformation process and our part in God's plan. God will be faithful to give us the gifts we need, *Jam 1:17-18, "Every good gift and every perfect gift is from above, and cometh down from the Father of lights, with whom is no variableness, neither shadow of turning. Of His own will begat He us with the word of truth, that we should be a kind of first fruits of His creatures."* Grace is one of His perfect gifts to us, exactly what we need. Now, we only need to accept it as His first fruits!

How do the devil and hell fit into God's plan?

God chose the best possible plan to create His eternal family and it included Lucifer, *Prov 16:4, "The Lord hath made all things for himself: yea, even the wicked for the day of evil."* So, God created Lucifer beautiful and talented; and God gave him one of the highest positions in Heaven, a covering Cherub. Lucifer's part in the plan is to present the best possible case for evil. God is playing Himself, the part of the purveyor of good, to offer us the choice between the two.

Lucifer allowed his beauty and lofty position to lead him to think himself worthy of replacing God. This vision of his glory turned Lucifer into Satan, the devil and God's counterpoint in this great mystery of Good and Evil, *Is 14:12-15, "How art thou fallen from heaven, O Lucifer, son of the morning! how art thou cut down to the ground, which didst weaken the nations! For thou hast said in thine heart, I will ascend into heaven, I will exalt my throne above the stars of God: I will sit also upon the mount of the congregation, in the sides of the north: I will ascend above the heights of the clouds; I will be like the most High. Yet thou shalt be brought down to hell, to the sides of the pit."* Isaiah describes the fall of Satan and prophesizes his final end. Lucifer was the first to think he does not need God. Satan has given us this virus, which continues to spread, and has so badly infected our world.

Satan, the devil, is the tragic figure who teaches all of us the ultimate ending for those who refuse to be part of God's eternal family. Ezekiel leads us on a journey from Lucifer to Satan. We see Lucifer's God given beauty and opportunities and how they are wasted in a life of evil punctuated by his attempts to destroy everything God is creating, *Eze 28:11-19, "Moreover the word of the Lord came unto me, saying, Son of man, take up a lamentation upon the king of Tyrus, and say unto him, Thus saith the Lord God; Thou sealest up the sum, full of wisdom, and perfect in beauty. Thou hast been in Eden the garden of God; every precious stone was thy covering, the sardius, topaz, and the diamond, the beryl, the onyx, and the jasper, the sapphire, the emerald, and the carbuncle, and gold: the workmanship of thy tabrets and of thy pipes was prepared in thee in the day that thou wast created. Thou art the anointed cherub that covereth; and I have set thee so: thou wast upon the holy mountain of God; thou hast walked up and down in the midst of the stones of fire. Thou wast perfect in thy ways from the day that thou wast created, till iniquity was found in thee. By the multitude of thy merchandise they have filled the midst of thee with violence, and thou hast sinned: therefore I will cast thee as profane out of the mountain of God: and I will destroy thee, O covering cherub, from the midst of the stones of fire.*

Thine heart was lifted up because of thy beauty, thou hast corrupted thy wisdom by reason of thy brightness: I will cast thee to the ground, I will lay thee before kings, that they may behold thee. Thou hast defiled thy sanctuaries by the multitude of thine iniquities, by the iniquity of thy traffick; therefore will I bring forth a fire from the midst of thee, it shall devour thee, and I will bring thee to ashes upon the earth in the sight of all them that behold thee. All they that know thee among the people shall be astonished at thee: thou shalt be a terror, and never shalt thou be any more." The path that Lucifer chose has only one ending, death. Until that death, he continues in his attempts to take as many of us as he can with him.

God is so confident in His plan that He allows the devil to work his evil in this world for two main reasons; to demonstrate how awful evil is and to provide the necessary contrast to the good He always offers, *Job 1:1, 12, 22, 42:7, "There was a man in the land of Uz, whose name was Job; and that man was perfect and upright, and one that feared God, and eschewed evil...And the Lord said unto Satan, Behold, all that he hath is in thy power; only upon himself put not forth thine hand. So Satan went forth from the presence of the Lord...In all this Job sinned not, nor charged God foolishly...And it was so, that after the Lord had spoken these words unto Job, the Lord said to Eliphaz the Temanite, My wrath is kindled against thee, and against thy two friends: for ye have not spoken of me the thing that is right, as my servant Job hath."* The devil used his evil ways to torment Job, in hopes that Job would then deny God, as so many had before and still do today. Job proved to be faithful and righteous, even when he lost everything and was suffering in pain. God is telling us to seek Him; no matter what the devil does to us and no matter how good things are for those who deny Him. And, to remind us that He does not bring us the suffering we are going through. We cannot let those who would blame God, instead of the devil, turn us away from God.

Rom 8:28, "And we know that all things work together for good to them that love God, to them who are the called according to his purpose." God is telling us that everything that happens is the result of the plan He chose to create His eternal family. God's plan takes into account the evil work of the devil and ends in good for those who love God. Sometimes, when we are in the middle of the darkness the devil is creating, it is hard to believe that good will somehow come from the evil the devil is spreading. My wife was listening to K-Love radio and Joshua Havens a former Starbucks barista told his story, how he had hoped to become a musician and it had not worked out, so he had to take a job as a barista. His faith in God is strong, so he was determined to be the best barista he could be. Then, God brought his future band members into Starbucks and the band The Afters was formed. God also brought his future wife into Starbucks! God's timing worked out for the best, because Joshua had faith in God's timing. When we are not willing to seek God in those dark days, the devil will enter and lead us further away from God. Then, sometimes the devil is able to use us to spread his evil. Believing in God allows us to understand that God loves us and gives us the ability to see past the evil, to be patient and wait for God's timing. This is when God is able to use us to spread His Truth!

In this life we struggle to understand the difference between good and evil. Some of us see this struggle as too much to bear, so we ignore it, or pretend there is no such thing as true good and true evil, and say that everything is relative. But, we are not struggling with the people we see committing evil acts, we are instead fighting with Satan and those he has convinced they should not accept God's offer of salvation, *Eph 6:12*, *"For we wrestle not against flesh and blood, but against principalities, against powers, against the rulers of the darkness of this world, against spiritual wickedness in high places."*

Zechariah tells us there are two possible outcomes, *Zech 13:9*, *"And I will bring the third part through the fire, and will refine them as silver is refined, and will try them as gold is tried: they shall call on my name, and I will hear them: I will say, It is my people: and they shall say, The Lord is my God."* We are either one of those who come through the fire to be God's children, or we will be destroyed in the same fire that will destroy Satan, which is hell, *Matt 3:11*, *"I indeed baptize you with water unto repentance. but he that cometh after me is mightier than I, whose shoes I am not worthy to bear: he shall baptize you with the Holy Ghost, and with fire:"* John the Baptist is telling us that Jesus will baptize us with the fire of the Holy Ghost. This is how we come through the fire. This is how we accept God's offer of salvation. Those who refuse God's offer will be left without an advocate at the judgment seat. Their ultimate destination is the second death, *Rev 20:15*, *"And whosoever was not found written in the book of life was cast into the lake of fire."* and *Rev 21:8*, *"But the fearful, and unbelieving, and the abominable, and murderers, and whoremongers, and sorcerers, and idolaters, and all liars, shall have their part in the lake which burneth with fire and brimstone: which is the second death."* This death is a second death, not an eternity spent burning in a fire.

Rev 21:1-3, "And I saw a new heaven and a new earth: for the first heaven and the first earth were passed away; and there was no more sea. And I John saw the holy city, new Jerusalem, coming down from God out of heaven, prepared as a bride adorned for her husband. And I heard a great voice out of heaven saying, Behold, the tabernacle of God is with men, and he will dwell with them, and they shall be his people, and God himself shall be with them, and be their God." Those who have accepted God's offer of salvation will live with Him in the Holy city, New Jerusalem. Those who have not accepted His offer will have died the second death in the lake of fire. They will be dead and will no longer feel pain, nor pleasure.

Hell then is not a place, it is the absence of God and consciousness, which the Bible calls the second death, *Eccl 9:5, "For the living know that they shall die: but the dead know not any thing, neither have they any more a reward; for the memory of them is forgotten."* and *Ps 115:17, "The dead praise not the Lord, neither any that go down into silence."* This is the end of God's plan; He will be with the living, those who have accepted His offer, *Matt 22:32, "I am the God of Abraham, and the God of Isaac, and the God of Jacob? God is not the God of the dead, but of the living."* God would prefer all would accept His offer, *Eze 33:11, "Say unto them, As I live, saith the Lord God, I have no pleasure in the death of the wicked; but that the wicked turn from his way and live: turn ye, turn ye from your evil ways; for why will ye die, O house of Israel?"*

Throughout all of history He has warned us about the fire that consumes those who refuse His offer. Even in the time of Moses the people misunderstood the fire, and the devil used their feelings of guilt to drive a wedge between them and God, *Deut 5:25, "Now therefore why should we die? for this great fire will consume us: if we hear the voice of the Lord our God any more, then we shall die."* Moses tried to help them understand God and reluctantly played the intermediary, even though he was frustrated by their lack of faith in the face of all they had seen God do. Today we have a very willing intermediary, Jesus, and all we need to do is accept Him as our savior. He is the way to a very personal eternity with God, *Jn 14:6, "Jesus saith unto him, I am the way, the truth, and the life: no man cometh unto the Father, but by me."*

We were created to be with God and those who choose to refuse to accept God's offer are already living in a hell of their own creation. The pain caused by their separation from God leads to all of the misery we witness every day; divorce, lies, murder, corruption, addictions, etc., *Eze 36:31, "Then shall ye remember your own evil ways, and your doings that were not good, and shall lothe yourselves in your own sight for your iniquities and for your abominations."* The people who have chosen this life only, will suffer the self-loathing it brings, the pain that results and so will those who come into contact with them.

The devil is just a player in the great mystery and hell is only the eternal separation from our creator, God.

God's plan is to use love and free will to allow each of us to choose to either accept His offer of salvation and eternal life with His eternal family; or to choose to live this life only. Each of us must choose for ourselves.

What Is God Doing To Complete His Plan?

When God saw the plan He was to choose to create His eternal family, He saw that it was divided into three distinct phases: Creation and His direct contact; prophets and His miracles; and finally, Jesus, His miracles, His Living Word, and the Holy Ghost.

Phase 1, Creation and His direct contact:

Gen 1:1, "In the beginning God created the heaven and the earth." God continued by creating humans and had a very personal relationship with them. He walked with them in the Garden of Eden, while teaching them all they needed to know to do their part in the plan He selected, *Gen 1:26, 2:15-16, 3:8, "And God said, Let us make man in our image, after our likeness: and let them have dominion over the fish of the sea, and over the fowl of the air, and over the cattle, and over all the earth, and over every creeping thing that creepeth upon the earth... And the Lord God took the man, and put him into the garden of Eden to dress it and to keep it. And the Lord God commanded the man, saying, Of every tree of the garden thou mayest freely eat: But of the tree of the knowledge of good and evil, thou shalt not eat of it: for in the day that thou eatest thereof thou shalt surely die... And they heard the voice of the Lord God walking in the garden in the cool of the day: and Adam and his wife hid themselves from the presence of the Lord God amongst the trees of the garden."* Adam and Eve disobeyed God and the resulting guilt caused them to hide from Him. All of human history will be about learning from this single mistake, over and over, again! Hiding from

God did not work then, and it will not work now. All things workout for the best when we reason with God, *Rom 8:28, "And we know that all things work together for good to them that love God, to them who are the called according to his purpose."* Too many people followed Adam and Eve's example, and it was time for God to step in and bring a new beginning from the good that had taken root.

So, in about 2,500 BC God began to transition from **Phase 1** to **Phase 2**, which became one of the defining moments in history, as God intervened by creating a worldwide flood that killed everyone except Noah and his family, separating the good, the wheat, from what had become an overwhelming amount of evil, the tares, *Gen 7:1, 16-19, "And the Lord said unto Noah, Come thou and all thy house into the ark; for thee have I seen righteous before me in this generation... And they that went in, went in male and female of all flesh, as God had commanded him: and the Lord shut him in. And the flood was forty days upon the earth; and the waters increased, and bare up the ark, and it was lift up above the earth. And the waters prevailed, and were increased greatly upon the earth; and the ark went upon the face of the waters. And the waters prevailed exceedingly upon the earth; and all the high hills, that were under the whole heaven, were covered."* This is the first of two times in all of history that God will separate the wheat from the tares. The next time will be at the completion of His plan. This was the end of **Phase 1,** and the era of prophets began.

Phase 2, Prophets and His miracles:

In **Phase 2** God stepped into the background, sending His prophets to communicate His plan and to prophesy future events.

Abraham was the first of the 57 prophets God sent in the Old Testament, here is the link: <u>The 57 Prophets God Sent</u>.[36] During **Phase 2** God used His miracles to fulfill those prophecies, providing the proof needed to authenticate the prophets He sent.

Amos 3:7, "Surely the Lord God will do nothing, but he revealeth his secret unto his servants the prophets." Amos is reporting what God had ordained; He will always warn us before He acts. He did this, in **Phase 2**, by speaking through His prophets.

Gen 12:1-2, 15:18, "Now the Lord had said unto Abram, Get thee out of thy country, and from thy kindred, and from thy father's house, unto a land that I will shew thee: And I will make of thee a great nation, and I will bless thee, and make thy name great; and thou shalt be a blessing:... In the same day the Lord made a covenant with Abram, saying, Unto thy seed have I given this land, from the river of Egypt unto the great river, the river Euphrates:" In 1947 Abram's prophecy was finally fulfilled, after nearly 1,800 years of exile, Israel was recreated to allow the Jewish people to return to the land God had promised them, over 3,500 years earlier. In 760 BC the prophet Amos refined the prophecy to include Israel remaining in this Promised Land until Jesus returns to complete God's plan, *Amos 9:15, "And I will plant them upon their land, and they shall no more be pulled up out of their land which I have given them, saith the Lord thy God."* Here is a link: <u>The Land God Promised The Jewish People</u>.[37] When we compare the map of the land God promised the Jews over 3,500 years ago to what they occupy today, can there be any doubt God ordained it? Against all odds and with enemies on all sides, Israel has withstood the onslaught from its neighbors. I remember how I felt in 1967 when I heard that Israel had staged a pre-emptive attack on Jordan, Syria and Egypt, who were closing in on Israel. In six days the war was over. I thought only a miracle could have made that possible. Here is a link to the details of that war: <u>The Story Of Six Day War</u>.[38] Israel continues today to survive attacks from multiple sources that wish death to this tiny country.

God gave Abraham another confirmation of a prior prophecy, *Gen 18:10, 21:2-3, "And he said, I will certainly return unto thee according to the time of life; and, lo, Sarah thy wife shall have a son. And Sarah heard it in the tent door, which was behind him... For Sarah conceived, and bare Abraham a son in his old age, at the set time of which God had spoken to him. And Abraham called the name of his son that was born unto him, whom Sarah bare to him, Isaac."* Abraham and Isaac formed the bloodline that produces the desired results, so God had to make sure that that bloodline was preserved.

In 1446 BC, when it was time for the Israelites to leave Egypt, God sent Moses to take them out of captivity with a whirlwind of miracles, *Ex 14:21-22, "And Moses stretched out his hand over the sea; and the Lord caused the sea to go back by a strong east wind all that night, and made the sea dry land, and the waters were divided. And the children of Israel went into the midst of the sea upon the dry ground: and the waters were a wall unto them on their right hand, and on their left."*

God had Moses deliver the Ten Commandments to us, *Ex 20:2-17, "I am the Lord thy God, which have brought thee out of the land of Egypt, out of the house of bondage. Thou shalt have no other gods before me. Thou shalt not make unto thee any graven image, or any likeness of any thing that is in heaven above, or that is in the earth beneath, or that is in the water under the earth. Thou shalt not bow down thyself to them, nor serve them: for I the Lord thy God am a jealous God, visiting the iniquity of the fathers upon the children unto the third and fourth generation of them that hate me; And shewing mercy unto thousands of them that love me, and keep my commandments. Thou shalt not take the name of the Lord thy God in vain; for the Lord will not hold him guiltless that taketh his name in vain. Remember the sabbath day, to keep it holy. Six days shalt thou labour, and do all thy work: But the seventh day is the sabbath of the Lord thy God: in it thou shalt not do any work, thou, nor thy son, nor thy daughter, thy manservant, nor thy maidservant, nor thy cattle, nor thy stranger that is within thy gates: For in six days the Lord made heaven and earth, the sea, and all that in them is, and rested the seventh day: wherefore the Lord blessed the sabbath day, and hallowed it. Honour thy father and thy mother: that thy days may be long upon the land which the Lord thy God giveth thee. Thou shalt not kill. Thou shalt not commit adultery. Thou shalt not steal. Thou shalt not bear false witness against thy neighbour. Thou shalt not covet thy neighbour's house, thou shalt not covet thy neighbour's wife, nor his manservant, nor his maidservant, nor his ox, nor his ass, nor any thing that is thy neighbour's."* In **Phase 1** God walked and talked with us, teaching these concepts directly. Now He would have His prophet give them to us again, this time in writing, so that future generations would be able to reason with Him.

David was a pivotal person in God's plan, so in 1024 BC God stepped in to make sure that David became a king, *1 Sam 17:47-50,* *"And all this assembly shall know that the Lord saveth not with sword and spear: for the battle is the Lord's, and he will give you into our hands. And it came to pass, when the Philistine arose, and came, and drew nigh to meet David, that David hastened, and ran toward the army to meet the Philistine. And David put his hand in his bag, and took thence a stone, and slang it, and smote the Philistine in his forehead, that the stone sunk into his forehead; and he fell upon his face to the earth. So David prevailed over the Philistine with a sling and with a stone, and smote the Philistine, and slew him; but there was no sword in the hand of David."* When David killed Goliath, his fame was sealed and the knowledge of the fact that God favored him was assured. The stone David sunk into Goliath's forehead was a foreshadowing of Jesus, for Jesus was the stone upon which God would built His church and the stone also represents His Word, which will sink into our minds. The bloodline to Jesus was again preserved!

Around 700 BC Isaiah foretold of Jesus' coming, *Is 9:6, "For unto us a child is born, unto us a son is given: and the government shall be upon his shoulder: and his name shall be called Wonderful, Counsellor, The mighty God, The everlasting Father, The Prince of Peace."* This is one of the signposts God left for Jesus to point to when He came, as proof of who He is. If only people would reason with Him.

In 622 BC God gave Jeremiah the task of reminding everyone who would listen, that God has a plan and anyone that follows it will be part of His eternal family, *Jer 11:1-4, "The word that came to Jeremiah from the Lord saying, Hear ye the words of this covenant, and speak unto the men of Judah, and to the inhabitants of Jerusalem; And say thou unto them, Thus saith the Lord God of Israel; Cursed be the man that* obeyeth not the words of this covenant, Which I commanded your fathers in the day that I brought them forth out of the land of Egypt, from the iron furnace, saying, Obey my voice, and do them, according to all which I command you: so shall ye be my people, and I will be your God:" This is not a new command, it is the same one He gave to Moses and it will be repeated many times over before the end comes.

In 592 BC God gave Ezekiel a furthering of the previous prophesy regarding the return of His people to Israel, *Eze 11:16-17,* *"Therefore say, Thus saith the Lord God; Although I have cast them far off among the heathen, and although I have scattered them among the countries, yet will I be to them as a little sanctuary in the countries where they shall come. Therefore say, Thus saith the Lord God; I will even gather you from the people, and assemble you out of the countries where ye have been scattered, and I will give you the land of Israel."* These people are the remnant that Ezekiel tells us about in, *Eze 6:8, "Yet will I leave a remnant, that ye may have some that shall escape the sword among the nations, when ye shall be scattered through the countries."* God tells us how we can know that someone is not a real prophet, *Deut 18:22,* *"When a prophet speaketh in the name of the Lord, if the thing follow not, nor come to pass, that is the thing which the Lord hath not spoken, but the prophet hath spoken it presumptuously: thou shalt not be afraid of him."* He also tells us how He communicates with real prophets, *Numb 12:6, "And he said, Hear now my words: If there be a prophet among you, I the Lord will make myself known unto him in a vision, and will speak unto him in a dream."* And, finally, He tells us that there will be many false prophets, *Matt 24:11, "And many false prophets shall rise, and shall deceive many."* Remember, a prophet is proven by the prophecies that come to pass.

There are more pre-Jesus prophets we could study, however, our time is limited and we now move on to **Phase 3**.

Phase 3, Jesus, His miracles, His Living Word, and the Holy Ghost:

We are living near the end of **Phase 3** of His plan. This is the phase where God completed His Living Word, which He intends for us to use to find Him and His love for us. Early in **Phase 3**, some walked and talked with Jesus, the rest of us are left with His Living Word and the Holy Ghost, to teach us the truth about this life and the next. There are no new prophecies in **Phase 3**; however, prophecies continue to be fulfilled that were made during **Phase 2**. Only a small percentage of all the prophecies ever made are yet to be fulfilled.

Heb 1:1-2, "God, who at sundry times and in divers manners spake in time past unto the fathers by the prophets, Hath in these last days spoken unto us by his Son, whom he hath appointed heir of all things, by whom also he made the worlds;" Paul is telling us that the time of the prophets ended and that it was marked by Jesus' ministry. The prophet's mission was to tell us about Jesus' coming, the purpose of His coming and what to expect during end times, *Eph 2:19-20, "Now therefore ye are no more strangers and foreigners, but fellowcitizens with the saints, and of the household of God; And are built upon the foundation of the apostles and prophets, Jesus Christ himself being the chief corner stone;"* Paul continues to explain that the foundation of God's church was now built upon the work of the apostles, the prophets and Jesus' Himself.

Lk 16:16, "The law and the prophets were until John: since that time the kingdom of God is preached, and every man presseth into it." Jesus left us with His Living Word, the Bible, so that we can reason with it and press on toward the kingdom of God. The Apostle John was the last prophet and he brought us the final book of the Bible, Revelation. Everyone else will only be repeating the prophecies we have received in the past, so that all may have the opportunity to hear them, or, they will be false prophets. He left us the Holy Ghost to guide us when we are sincere in our reasoning, so that we might recognize the false prophets.

Those who actually witnessed Jesus' miracles documented them in the scriptures. We do not have time to review all of them, however, the personal testimony of the miracle that transformed Saul into Paul is extremely important, *Acts 9:4-5, 18-20, "And he fell to the earth, and heard a voice saying unto him, Saul, Saul, why persecutest thou me? And he said, Who art thou, Lord? And the Lord said, I am Jesus whom thou persecutest: it is hard for thee to kick against the pricks...And immediately there fell from his eyes as it had been scales: and he received sight forthwith, and arose, and was baptized. And when he had received meat, he was strengthened. Then was Saul certain days with the disciples which were at Damascus. And straightway he preached Christ in the synagogues, that he is the Son of God."*

Acts 14:17, "Yet he has not left himself without testimony: He has shown kindness by giving you rain from heaven and crops in their seasons;

he provides you with plenty of food and fills your hearts with joy." God communicates with us many ways each day. He asks us to pay attention and understand that He wants all of us to accept His invitation to spend eternity with Him. The proof of this is the testimony of those who have personally witnessed His miracles.

Having an eternal perspective on things we do in this life is not normal for us. We are more interested in immediate gratification. Accepting God's gift allows our selfish nature to fade in the light of God's love, as we then begin the transformation that leads us to follow His eternal Truth to our better self. Our selfless self!

Are we really in the middle of a battle between Good And Evil? First we need to get a handle on definitions, as defined by dictionary.com. A Battle is: a hostile encounter or engagement between opposing military forces; participation in such hostile encounters or engagements; a fight between two persons or animals; any conflict or struggle. Good is: morally excellent; virtuous; righteous; pious; satisfactory in quality, quantity, or degree; of high quality; excellent; right; proper; fit; well behaved; kind, beneficent, or friendly; honorable or worthy; in good standing. Evil is: morally wrong or bad; immoral; wicked; harmful; injurious; characterized or accompanied by misfortune or suffering; unfortunate; disastrous; due to actual or imputed bad conduct or character; marked by anger, irritability, irascibility.

Reading the headlines in any newspaper today should answer our question. The headlines are full of reports of crime, corruption, hatred, terrorism, rape, human trafficking, and every other kind of evil known to mankind. These sound like hostile encounters. What gives these people the right to do these things? Are Christians being targeted? Are we involved in a battle? Some might characterize this battle as one of freedoms, some wanting to be able to do whatever they want and some wanting to be safe from the deeds of those very same people. But, the Bible tells us we can know the one we follow by observing the nature of the fruits of our actions, *Matt 7:17, "Even so every good tree bringeth forth good fruit; but a corrupt tree bringeth forth evil fruit."* Either we are following God and His good ways, or we are following the devil and his evil ways. God has warned us about these days, *2 Tim 3:1-2, "This know also, that in the last days perilous times shall come. For men shall be lovers of their own selves, covetous, boasters, proud, blasphemers, disobedient to parents, unthankful, unholy,"* Imagine for the moment what life would be like with someone like Satan in charge. No one would be free; no one would be happy, not even Satan.

"Two paths, leading in opposite directions, call us to our ultimate destination. Two beings wait at the end of these paths, both calling for us to come to them. Each path draws us with what appear to be similar lures, and each has its own rewards along the way. But, they have very different final destinations...God calls us from the path that leads to Good and eternal life. The devil calls us from the path that leads to Evil, and ultimately death." To read the complete "Story of Good and Evil", use this link to download a free copy: Good and Evil.[39]

The simple truth of the question of good and evil is that those who choose to do good do it out of love, *Matt 5:44*, *"But I say unto you, Love your enemies, bless them that curse you, do good to them that hate you, and pray for them which despitefully use you, and persecute you;"* Those who choose to do evil do it out of self-love. Love says that we care about others, to the extent we are willing to think of their needs above our own, even willing to die for them, *Jn 15:13*, *"Greater love hath no man than this, that a man lay down his life for his friends."* Therefore, when it comes time to choose what to do in any situation, love causes us to choose the right thing, even when it does not produce the best outcome for us. Conversely, self-love puts our interests ahead of everyone else's and whenever there is a decision to be made, we pick our own interests.

So, the politician who lies to gain office cares little for those being hurt by the lie, *Jn 8:44*, *"Ye are of your father the devil, and the lusts of your father ye will do. He was a murderer from the beginning, and abode not in the truth, because there is no truth in him. When he speaketh a lie, he speaketh of his own: for he is a liar, and the father of it."* The terrorist does not think about those innocent people being killed. The rapist does not care about the physical and mental pain they cause their victims. Many times the act of rape is not about sex, it is about control and the need of the rapist to feel that control. It is a selfish act. Do these horrible actions sound like they come from God, or the devil?

The ultimate definition of evil is the absence of good. Much like darkness is the absence of light. You cannot add more darkness to overcome the light; you can only cover up the light, or Truth, thus reducing the light, which allows darkness to fill the void, *Acts 26:18-20, "But rise, and stand upon thy feet: for I have appeared unto thee for this purpose, to make thee a minister and a witness both of these things which thou hast seen, and of those things in the which I will appear unto thee; Delivering thee from the people, and from the Gentiles, unto whom now I send thee, To open their eyes, and to turn them from darkness to light, and from the power of Satan unto God, that they may receive forgiveness of sins, and inheritance among them which are sanctified by faith that is in me."* When people doing good step in to stop evil, evil runs. Why? Because doing evil is a cowardly act. When people inclined to do evil have no power, they are more than willing to seem reasonable. They still want to do evil and are waiting for an advantage to appear. But, give those same people some power and watch how much evil they do and how little those people care about the suffering of others. Cowards act only when they see no immediate threat to doing their evil deeds. Picture the final moments before good closed in on Hitler and Sadam Hussein. Hitler was hiding in his bunker and killed himself, while Sadam was hiding in a hole in the ground. Do they sound like great warriors of good, or cowards? Links to these two events: Hitler's death.[40] and Saddam's capture.[41]

Why would anyone pick the side of evil, if this path really does exist? The answer has been complicated by the devil. His way is to confuse us so that we cannot see the Truth, *1 Cor 14:33, "For God is not the author of confusion, but of peace, as in all churches of the saints."*

God's way is speaking the truth, simply and honestly, *2 Cor 1:12*, *"For our rejoicing is this, the testimony of our conscience, that in simplicity and godly sincerity, not with fleshly wisdom, but by the grace of God, we have had our conversation in the world, and more abundantly to you-ward."* The devil hopes to keep us from the Truth. So, how does the devil keep us from the Truth?

The devil first tries to keep us from God's Truth by destroying God's Word, either by getting rid of Bibles or producing false religions, *Matt 7:15, "Beware of false prophets, which come to you in sheep's clothing, but inwardly they are ravening wolves."* Secondly, he tries to make us think that God did not mean what he said, *Gen 3:1 "Now the serpent was more subtil than any beast of the field which the Lord God had made. And he said unto the woman, Yea, hath God said, Ye shall not eat of every tree of the garden?"* If these two ways are unsuccessful, he works on our ego, in an attempt to make us think we are smarter than God, *Lk 4:3-4, "And the devil said unto him, If thou be the Son of God, command this stone that it be made bread. And Jesus answered him, saying, It is written, That man shall not live by bread alone, but by every word of God."* If that does not work he makes us so busy that we do not have time to read the Truth, nor to reason with God, *Lk 10:40-42, "But Martha was cumbered about much serving, and came to him, and said, Lord, dost thou not care that my sister hath left me to serve alone? bid her therefore that she help me. And Jesus answered and said unto her, Martha, Martha, thou art careful and troubled about many things: But one thing is needful: and Mary hath chosen that good part, which shall not be taken away from her."* In his final attempts, he will bring us every kind of sinful distraction, hoping to find the addiction within us waiting to appear. It could be the lust for money, sex, power, drugs, etc., *1 Jn 2:16, "For all that is in the world, the lust of the flesh, and the lust of the eyes, and the pride of life, is not of the Father, but is of the world."* God has warned us about evil and all of the devil's schemes! *Prov 8:13, "The fear of the Lord is to hate evil: pride, and arrogancy, and the evil way, and the froward mouth, do I hate."*

Nah 1:11,13, "There is one come out of thee, that imagineth evil against the Lord, a wicked counsellor...For now will I break his yoke from off thee, and will burst thy bonds in sunder." The devil and his workers are always counseling us to defy God. Reasoning with God produces the best answers, *1 Thes 5:21, "Prove all things; hold fast that which is good."* and *3 Jn 1:11, "Beloved, follow not that which is evil, but that which is good. He that doeth good is of God: but he that doeth evil hath not seen God."* There certainly seems to be a distinction between good and evil, and doing good is God's way, *Ps 5:4, "For thou art not a God that hath pleasure in wickedness: neither shall evil dwell with thee."* God avoids evil; He will not allow it to dwell with Him.

Why does the devil make the mistake of opposing God? *Is 14:12-18, "How art thou fallen from heaven, O Lucifer, son of the morning! how art thou cut down to the ground, which didst weaken the nations! For thou hast said in thine heart, I will ascend into heaven, I will exalt my throne above the stars of God: I will sit also upon the mount of the congregation, in the sides of the north:"* Satan wants the glory he envies when he sees God. The very reason Satan makes this mistake is the same one keeping him from understanding why he is making it. Satan is so selfish; he cannot imagine a reluctant leader, ruling only because there is not a better being to take His place.

When we stop trying to make God into something He is not and start understanding that He loves us and wants only the best for us, we will stop making The Satan Mistake! We could continue to live our lives as though this is not important, as if there is not a battle being waged, but that is exactly what Satan wants us to do. The solution is to read the Bible, pray and start living our lives like we believe there is a God! *Ps 18:30, "As for God, his way is perfect: the word of the Lord is tried: he is a buckler to all those that trust in him."*

If this is not a battle, why are so many people harming Christians? Links to articles: Bible Translators Killed[42]; Water Tower With Church Name[43]; Christians Targeted For Extermination[44]; Christians Targeted By Oregon Shooter[45]; Easter Bombing[46]...I could show thousands more of these kinds of articles. Satan wants every sign of Christ and every person that believes in Christ removed from this world! Does anything else make sense? How many Christians, today, are targeting another group? I know some of us want to paint everything done, in the name of Christianity as proof against the religion. But, not everyone that claims to be a Christian is one. Christ Himself told us this, *Matt 7:21, "Not every one that saith unto me, Lord, Lord, shall enter into the kingdom of heaven; but he that doeth the will of my Father which is in heaven."* The actions of these false Christians are the work of Satan; who is trying again to drive a wedge between God and us. God never calls us to harm anyone! Remember, He told us to look to their fruit to know the truth! If these false Christians are doing things contrary to God's Word, they are not Christians! He wants us to overcome evil with good, Rom 12:21, *"Be not overcome of evil, but overcome evil with good."*

God wants all to have the opportunity to come to Him and share in the love of the eternal family, 2 Pet 3:9, *"The Lord is not slack concerning his promise, as some men count slackness; but is longsuffering to us-ward, not willing that any should perish, but that all should come to repentance."* His patience provides us the time we need to understand and choose His love. He would prefer for everyone to choose to come to Him, Lk 15:4-6, *"What man of you, having an hundred sheep, if he lose one of them, doth not leave the ninety and nine in the wilderness, and go after that which is lost, until he find it? And when he hath found it, he layeth it on his shoulders, rejoicing. And when he cometh home, he calleth together his friends and neighbours, saying unto them, Rejoice with me; for I have found my sheep which was lost."* He is doing all He can to draw all of us to Him, every single one of us.

He gives good gifts to His children. He never changes and always cares about us, because He loves all of us. This is how we know that Heaven will be a very special place, Jam 1:17-18, *"Every good gift and every perfect gift is from above, and cometh down from the Father of lights, with whom is no variableness, neither shadow of turning. Of His own will begat He us with the word of truth, that we should be a kind of first fruits of His creatures."* Jesus is the Truth, the way, and the first fruit of the first death.

God watches as His family experiences the pain of this world, much like a husband watches his wife during labor. Both know the family being born is worth all the pain the process brings, *Rom 8:22*, *"For we know that the whole creation groaneth and travaileth in pain together until now."* Then, suddenly, in the twinkling of an eye, all will change, *1 Cor 15:52*, *"In a moment, in the twinkling of an eye, at the last trump: for the trumpet shall sound, and the dead shall be raised incorruptible, and we shall be changed."* Our Lord will take us home, *Rev 21:3-4*, *"And I heard a great voice out of heaven saying, Behold, the tabernacle of God is with men, and he will dwell with them, and they shall be his people, and God himself shall be with them, and be their God. And God shall wipe away all tears from their eyes; and there shall be no more death, neither sorrow, nor crying, neither shall there be any more pain: for the former things are passed away."* Yes, the birthing process truly represents the creation of God's own eternal family.

Why does God teach us to treat everyone with love, even our enemies? *Matt 5:44-45*, *"But I say unto you, Love your enemies, bless them that curse you, do good to them that hate you, and pray for them which despitefully use you, and persecute you; That ye may be the children of your Father which is in heaven: for He maketh his sun to rise on the evil and on the good, and sendeth rain on the just and on the unjust."* He does this because He wants us to know what we can expect in Heaven. If we cannot forgive, we will hate Heaven. If we cannot love everyone, we will hate Heaven. If we are selfish and think of ourselves first, we will hate Heaven. God is always truthful and more than willing to communicate with us, *Lk 14:35*, *"He that hath ears to hear, let him hear."*

This is the plan He has been working on for thousands of years; first directly, then through the prophets, next by Jesus, and now finally, by the Bible and the Holy Ghost, who is with us until Jesus' return to collect His family. The truth has always been with us and His story has never changed. He wants an eternal family, He continues do everything He needs to do to make it happen, and Heaven is ready for us. Are we ready for Heaven?

Who Are We?

Are we who we think we are, who we want to be, who we pretend to be, or maybe we are who other people think we are?

Thinking, wanting, or pretending does not change who we are. God sees through all of these possibilities to the truth of who we really are! So, why are we wasting so many of our precious resources trying to be somebody else? In case some are wondering, those precious resources are our time, money and energy. What would happen if we used all of these resources to accelerate the process of becoming the person we were created capable of becoming? What has been the emotional cost of all of this pretending?

The Bible tells us we are God's created beings, made in His image. *Gen 1:26-28, "And God said, Let us make man in our image, after our likeness: and let them have dominion over the fish of the sea, and over the fowl of the air, and over the cattle, and over all the earth, and over every creeping thing that creepeth upon the earth. So God created man in his own image, in the image of God created he him; male and female created he them. And God blessed them, and God said unto them, Be fruitful, and multiply, and replenish the earth, and subdue it: and have dominion over the fish of the sea, and over the fowl of the air, and over every living thing that moveth upon the earth."*

Gen 2:7, "And the Lord God formed man of the dust of the ground, and breathed into his nostrils the breath of life; and man became a living soul." God placed His Spirit into the beings He created and created living souls, *Eze 18:4, Behold, all souls are mine; as the soul of the father, so also the soul of the son is mine: the soul that sinneth, it shall die.*" Without the breath of life He gave us, we die. If we die without a savior, we will face the second death, for God will not allow sin to enter the New Jerusalem.

We have the opportunity to move from created beings to God's children, *Matt 12:50, For whosoever shall do the will of my Father which is in heaven, the same is my brother, and sister, and mother.*" So, we have to do the will of God the Father to become His adopted children. *Heb 11:6, "But without faith it is impossible to please him: for he that cometh to God must believe that he is, and that he is a rewarder of them that diligently seek him."* Thus, we learn that we cannot do the will of God the Father if we do not believe He exists, *Matt 23:9, "And call no man your father upon the earth: for one is your Father, which is in heaven."* and *1 Jn 3:1, "Behold, what manner of love the Father hath bestowed upon us, that we should be called the sons of God: therefore the world knoweth us not, because it knew him not."*

Our first birth is as created beings into this sinful world and our second birth is our moving from created beings into children of God and members of His eternal family, *Jn 3:3, "Jesus answered and said unto him, Verily, verily, I say unto thee, Except a man be born again, he cannot see the kingdom of God."* Jesus is telling us that if we are not born again, we will not see the kingdom of God in this world, nor the next. If we do not see the kingdom of God in this world, we will not do the work God has given us to do in this life. Without the vision of God's kingdom we will not be able to follow His Commandments. It is the following of His Commandments that shows the world that God is alive in us and serves as a light to draw them to reason with God. This reasoning is their opportunity to be born again.

John the Baptist explained the difference between baptism before and after Jesus' ministry in, *Matt 3:11, "I indeed baptize you with water unto repentance: but he that cometh after me is mightier than I, whose shoes I am not worthy to bear: he shall baptize you with the Holy Ghost, and with fire:"* When we accept Jesus as our savior we can clearly hear the Comforter God has sent us, the Holy Ghost, who dwells within us and helps us reason with His Living Word, *Jn 14:26, "But the Comforter, which is the Holy Ghost, whom the Father will send in my name, he shall teach you all things, and bring all things to your remembrance, whatsoever I have said unto you."* Our reasoning with God turns our lukewarm understanding of Him into a fire for His Truth.

God wants us to build our lives on solid ground, *Matt 7:24, "Therefore whosoever heareth these sayings of mine, and doeth them, I will liken him unto a wise man, which built his house upon a rock:"* When we build our lives on the rock that is God and His wisdom, we will not be swayed by the tide of current opinions and fleshy wisdom. We will work toward that perfect version of ourselves. We will not feel we need to invent new philosophies to show others how smart we are, instead we will follow the never changing wisdom of God.

2 Tim 3:16-17, "All scripture is given by inspiration of God, and is profitable for doctrine, for reproof, for correction, for instruction in righteousness: That the man of God may be perfect, thoroughly furnished unto all good works." We have the potential of becoming perfect and the closer we come to perfect the bigger the percentage of what we do will be good works! *Eph 4:15, "But speaking the truth in love, may grow up into him in all things, which is the head, even Christ:"* Once we accept Jesus and begin reasoning with His Word, we need to speak the truth in love, no matter what the cost! This means we do not force anyone to do anything. We only communicate what God has told us and let everyone make his or her own decisions. Then, we love them no matter what they decide to do. Without free will there is no love, *1 Jn 4:18, "There is no fear in love; but perfect love casteth out fear: because fear hath torment. He that feareth is not made perfect in love."* We can be made perfect in love.

We have been born into a world that is rushing to kill God. Fear not, God is safe and those who are trying to kill Him will end up falling on their own sword, which means they will succeed only in killing their opportunity of having God living within them. God's sword is His Living Word; those who choose another sword will find their sword their downfall, *Job 36:12, "But if they obey not, they shall perish by the sword, and they shall die without knowledge."* God's Living Word is the sword of knowledge that saves us from all other swords.

Once we begin reasoning with the Living Word, we can count on God to continue the work of moving us toward our perfect version, *Phil 1:6*, *"Being confident of this very thing, that he which hath begun a good work in you will perform it until the day of Jesus Christ:"* When we move toward perfect, people can count on us, *Acts 24:16*, *"And herein do I exercise myself, to have always a conscience void to offence toward God, and toward men."* We will speak the Truth that God has given us, every time. We will look forward to the day we will hear our Lord say, *Matt 25:23*, *"His lord said unto him, Well done, good and faithful servant; thou hast been faithful over a few things, I will make thee ruler over many things: enter thou into the joy of thy lord."*

So, being God's children, what shall we do to demonstrate who we are? Once we believe in the Living Word, we are meant to be fruitful and pass it on to others, *Matt 13:18-23*, *"Hear ye therefore the parable of the sower. When any one heareth the word of the kingdom, and understandeth it not, then cometh the wicked one, and catcheth away that which was sown in his heart. This is he which received seed by the way side. But he that received the seed into stony places, the same is he that heareth the word, and anon with joy receiveth it; Yet hath he not root in himself, but dureth for a while: for when tribulation or persecution ariseth because of the word, by and by he is offended. He also that received seed among the thorns is he that heareth the word; and the care of this world, and the deceitfulness of riches, choke the word, and he becometh unfruitful. But he that received seed into the good ground is he that heareth the word, and understandeth it; which also beareth fruit, and bringeth forth, some an hundredfold, some sixty, some thirty."* If we hide our faith by not allowing anyone to see we believe in God, we cannot do our part in giving everyone the opportunity to choose eternal life with God. So, it is by our doing our part in spreading the Truth, that we finish His work. Our part could be serving others, teaching children, helping the sick, assisting a widow in her time of trouble, witnessing to others, preaching to others, evangelizing, etc. God has given each of us very special and unique gifts, and when we use these gifts to become the person God created us to be, people will notice God in our actions. Some of the people in our lives will not have a better opportunity to see God at work, than they will when they witness our work.

All of God's actions are measured. He has a plan and is actively working to complete it. We are made in His image and He wants us to take the measured actions He has demonstrated for us by His Word and His actions. He has parts for each of us in His plan, if we choose to accept His offer. Some of us are to influence millions, like the apostles. Some of us are to help influence just one person. He wants everyone to have the opportunity to accept His offer. When we go to God in prayer, He will direct us to the correct path for our lives, *Prov 4:26, "Ponder the path of thy feet, and let all thy ways be established. Turn not to the right hand nor to the left: remove thy foot from evil."* If we do not work to complete our parts in His plan, others will try to force us to work on their plans. The devil is behind all of these attempts to control us, to make us slaves in his battle against God. *1 Pet 5:8, "Be sober, be vigilant; because your adversary the devil, as a roaring lion, walketh about, seeking whom he may devour:"* Many will ignore His guidance and follow their own path, *Prov 14:12, "There is a way which seemeth right unto a man, but the end thereof are the ways of death."*

So, what does the fruit God calls us to produce look like? *Gal 5:22-23, "But the fruit of the Spirit is love, joy, peace, longsuffering, gentleness, goodness, faith, Meekness, temperance: against such there is no law."* If we are willing to live the fruitful life God is calling us to, we must first decide to accept Jesus' offer of salvation. Every other choice we make will be affected by this one choice! How are the rest of our choices affected by our decision to accept Jesus as our savior?

The Bible tells us that the key to understanding the manual God has left for us is faith, and that it is impossible for us to understand His manual without faith, *Heb 11:6, "But without faith it is impossible to please him: for he that cometh to God must believe that he is, and that he is a rewarder of them that diligently seek him. By faith Noah, being warned of God of things not seen as yet, moved with fear, prepared an ark to the saving of his house; by the which he condemned the world, and became heir of the righteousness which is by faith."* If we have not chosen to believe, we will not be able to accept the Truth of the Bible and therefore, we will not seek Him, we will not be able to accept His advice, and we will not be able to build our arks, nor will we be fruitful. It is this faith growing into maturity that helps us continue to peel back the layers in the Bible, rewarding us with an ever deeper understanding of God's will for us.

Everyday we have an unlimited number of choices to make. We can call in sick and go back to bed. We can take our kids out to throw around a baseball after work. We can call home and see if our spouse needs us to pick up anything on the way home. We can plan a robbery, or go to a bar and drink until we cannot remember how we got home. And the list goes on and on and on.

So, how do we know which of the unlimited number of choices are the right ones? Looking at the state of the world we live in, I would say it is very difficult to choose correctly, on our own. But, fortunately for us, God has already written a manual that helps us choose correctly, every time! The Bible, *Prov 3:5-6, "Trust in the Lord with all thine heart; and lean not unto thine own understanding. In all thy ways acknowledge him, and he shall direct thy paths."* Becoming whole and the person we were created to be is a very complicated process. Only God knows the future, but He has promised us that all things work together for good to them that love God, *Tit 3:8, "This is a faithful saying, and these things I will that thou affirm constantly, that they which have believed in God might be careful to maintain good works. These things are good and profitable unto men."* He makes this complicated world very simple, *Matt 6:33, "But seek ye first the kingdom of God, and his righteousness; and all these things shall be added unto you."*

When we do not believe in God, we will figure out a way to rationalize every decision we make, for everything then becomes relative. We will figure out a way to blame others for everything bad that happens in our lives, for without God's Word living within us, we think we are good and certainly not responsible for the bad things that happen. Each person's whim becomes everyone else's mandate. So, we have people trying to change what is legal for everyone else, to fit their personal mandate, *Prov 21:2, "Every way of a man is right in his own eyes: but the Lord pondereth the hearts."* This is not an action that demonstrates a spirit of love. Remember, God is love and free will is at the heart of all decisions we should make. We therefore care about how our choices limit the choices of others. We take responsibility for the things we do, rather than blaming others. Making the choice to go our own way, instead of following God's advice, might work for a moment or two; however, eventually the guilt will begin to work on our conscience, *Ps 14:2,* *"The Lord looks down from heaven on all mankind to see if there are any who understand, any who seek God."* The feeling of God watching us will shine a strong light on everything we do and ultimately we will see the good and the evil we have done in our lives. The clarity brought at that moment, will provide us with an opportunity to remove our feet from evil.

The Bible is full of stories about people who followed, and refused to follow, God's advice. Reading *Genesis Chapters 37-50* brings us the story of Joseph, who always put God above all else, leaving greed, power, and selfishness behind. Each time his faithfulness was tested and he proved to be faithful; something came along which made his future seem bleak. However, God always provided a way out of trouble and God's way eventually brought Joseph to the second most powerful position in all of Egypt, second only to Pharaoh. Joseph trusted God and God rewarded Joseph with the life God had created him capable of living. This is how God's timing makes all things work together for good. We just need to learn to be patient enough to wait for God's timing, *Eccl 3:1,*

"To every thing there is a season, and a time to every purpose under the heaven:" and *Ps 27:14, "Wait on the Lord: be of good courage, and he shall strengthen thine heart: wait, I say, on the Lord."*

One day we will all face God at the judgment seat. Some will be very confident as they step before God, only to find that they had not followed God, but some version of God that suited them. This will be a very bleak moment for them, *Matt 7:22-23, "Many will say to me in that day, Lord, Lord, have we not prophesied in thy name? and in thy name have cast out devils? and in thy name done many wonderful works? And then will I profess unto them, I never knew you: depart from me, ye that work iniquity."* and *Heb 11:6, "But without faith it is impossible to please him: for he that cometh to God must believe that he is, and that he is a rewarder of them that diligently seek him."*

In this life, the only choice that really matters is faith in God! *Jn 3:33, "He that hath received his testimony hath set to his seal that God is true."*

We are meant to work toward perfection in this life, *Phil 3:12-15, "Not as though I had already attained, either were already perfect: but I follow after, if that I may apprehend that for which also I am apprehended of Christ Jesus. Brethren, I count not myself to have apprehended: but this one thing I do, forgetting those things which are behind, and reaching forth unto those things which are before, I press toward the mark for the prize of the high calling of God in Christ Jesus. Let us therefore, as many as be perfect, be thus minded: and if in any thing ye be otherwise minded, God shall reveal even this unto you."* Paul, with Timothy's help, is telling us that the prize we are working to receive is the high calling of God in Christ. This life is the race we are to run toward perfection. When believers disagree on a topic, they are to discuss it and go to God, who will reveal the truth of the matter, *Is 1:18, "Come now, and let us reason together, saith the Lord: though your sins be as scarlet, they shall be as white as snow; though they be red like crimson, they shall be as wool."* This is how we reason with God and transform into the being He created us capable of becoming.

When I read the following quote in Mere Christianity by CS Lewis I was startled into reasoning with God; "I am trying here to prevent anyone saying the really foolish thing that people often say about Him: I am ready to accept Jesus as a great moral teacher, but I do not accept his claim to be God. That is the one thing we must not say. A man who was merely a man and said the sort of things Jesus said would not be a great moral teacher. He would either be a lunatic — on the level with the man who says he is a poached egg — or else he would be the Devil of Hell. You must make your choice. Either this man was, and is, the Son of God, or else a madman or something worse. You can shut him up for a fool, you can spit at him and kill him as a demon or you can fall at his feet and call him Lord and God, but let us not come with any patronizing nonsense about his being a great human teacher. He has not left that open to us. He did not intend to." Some agnostics and atheists claim that CS Lewis is not presenting all of the options for Jesus claims of being the Son of God. I disagree, after spending many years pondering his quote, in the light of the Bible; I have come to agree that there are no other options. To dispute that Jesus claimed He is the Son of God, would be to admit that we have not read the Bible. But, those who have read the Bible know better, *Matt 16:16-17, "And Simon Peter answered and said, Thou art the Christ, the Son of the living God. And Jesus answered and said unto him, Blessed art thou, Simon Barjona: for flesh and blood hath not revealed it unto thee, but my Father which is in heaven."*

I spent the next thirteen years, after reading the CS Lewis quote, reasoning with God, which ended with my baptism. It has been another fourteen years, since my baptism, and I have been running the race ever since. Running the race means reasoning with God and paying attention to what we actually do in this world. One by one, as a result of this process, I have changed many of those things I did in the past. When I finally realize that something I have been doing is wrong, I admit my mistake by confessing my sin to those affected, work to develop habits that will make the repeating of the mistake less likely and pray for God's help. This is how we change, *Rom 12:2, "And be not conformed to this world: but be ye transformed by the renewing of your mind, that ye may prove what is that good, and acceptable, and perfect, will of God."*

It is rather amazing to look back and see how unaware I was of what I was doing and how those actions were affecting the people I love. It is so easy to get locked into self and ignore others. But, God is faithful and will provide a way for those willing to let the light of His Truth shine on their lives. Introspection can be a painful process. It requires us to see our own faults. But, if we are to change, we must first be willing to admit we are not perfect and to demonstrate the willingness to change, *2 Cor 3:12, 18, "Seeing then that we have such hope, we use great plainness of speech...But we all, with open face beholding as in a glass the glory of the Lord, are changed into the same image from glory to glory, even as by the Spirit of the Lord."*

My confession is that it is worth the effort! My testimony is that the truth that God exists becomes ever more evident once we begin this process. On my journey God has provided many paths that would have been impossible to find without Him. Too many things have happened to me over the past twenty-seven years, which would have fallen into the impossible category, to believe they were products of random events, *Matt 19:26, "But Jesus beheld them, and said unto them, With men this is impossible; but with God all things are possible."* When we are in pursuit of God's plan for our lives, everything keeps getting easier.

When I was young you might have labeled me an existentialist. I believed you made your own way in life and that there were no right choices, just the ones you decided on. The one anchor that held me from adopting this philosophy entirely was my grandmother. The most wonderful person I knew and a devote Catholic. She believed in Jesus and at the time I thought it was quaint. An existentialist is not necessarily an atheist, so I was on the fence about God. Here is a link to an eight-minute video on existentialism: What Is Existentialism?[47] My journey has led me past the cynical idea that there is no moral right. I have seen too many people choosing to do things their own way and the disastrous results of their actions. Only when we add God and His moral code to our lives do we move toward Him and His purpose for all that He has created. Then, we can understand this world and the evil that persists, *Gal 1:4, "Who gave himself for our sins, that he might deliver us from this present evil world, according to the will of God and our Father:"* No life makes sense when it is examined in the light of His Truth, except the one that God has foreseen. Remember, we are all created with free will and consequently, not all will choose to follow God to the eternal future He is offering. This produces two basic paths for our lives; towards God and the eternal life He has promised, or away from God to the death He has warned us about. We can witness the truth of these two paths being played out in our world today, if we honestly examine this world and the things people willingly do.

Jean Paul Sartre, Albert Camus, Soren Kierkegaard, Friedrich Nietzsche, and the rest of the great thinkers who have tried to lead us away from God have missed the common element that proves their conclusions are incorrect, the inherent love we each have for other people. This inherent love draws us to sacrifice our lives for others; it draws us to devote our lives to curing diseases, feeding the homeless, caring for the orphans, draws us together when tragic events occur like the shooting in an Orlando nightclub, etc. It is God and His love that resides in each of us that causes us to do these things. Existentialism is at its heart selfish, "I know better;" while God's love at its heart selfless, "I am made to serve." *Gal 5:13, "For, brethren, ye have been called unto liberty; only use not liberty for an occasion to the flesh, but by love serve one another."*

The results of God moving in my life have been a more peaceful life, better relationships with family and friends, a better vision of what God wants me to do and where this world is headed. When I see the headlines of current events, I am no longer wondering what is going on, everything that is happening is in alignment with what God has seen and told us in the Bible. God is a gentle being who has provided a way for each of us to run our race in this world. It is up to each of us to make our own decision, *Joel 3:14, "Multitudes, multitudes in the valley of decision: for the day of the Lord is near in the valley of decision."* God allows each of us to make our own decision and this is love in its purest form.

So, the conclusion of the matter is that once we accept Jesus as our savior, we continue to move toward Him. We give up, one by one, the actions that lead away from Him. We come to reason with Him daily, or as close to daily as we can. We pray for guidance and open our hearts and minds to the Holy Ghost who is working so hard to help us understand the Truth of His Living Word, *Jn 14:26, "But the Comforter, which is the Holy Ghost, whom the Father will send in my name, he shall teach you all things, and bring all things to your remembrance, whatsoever I have said unto you."* We learn to love and serve, to empathize without judging, and to conform our lives to the vision God has for us. This becomes our life-long pursuit.

Can we avoid making a real decision about God?

It would be nice to go through this life without the cares of this world weighing us down. We would be able to live like children playing games everyday, becoming Peter Pan. However, there is evil in this world which will eventually prey on our innocence, if we pretend that it does not exist, *1 Pet 5:8, "Be sober, be vigilant; because your adversary the devil, as a roaring lion, walketh about, seeking whom he may devour:"* The devil is seeking whom he may devour, now that sounds ominous!

The heart of the problem is that none of us are perfect, yet! We have all sinned, *Rom 3:23, "For all have sinned, and come short of the glory of God;"* Which means we all have weaknesses that the devil will eventually discover and use to drive a wedge between God and us. Once he is successful, our only way out of that addiction is with God's help. This is why successful addiction programs include the belief in a higher power, early in their processes. This step works because to break free from addictions we have to first stop relying on our own efforts, for we are not fighting against flesh and blood, *Eph 6:12, "For we wrestle not against flesh and blood, but against principalities, against powers, against the rulers of the darkness of this world, against spiritual wickedness in high places."* We will not be able to withstand these spiritual attacks on our own.

This is why God has given us a way out of every temptation the devil brings to us, *1 Cor 10:13, "There hath no temptation taken you but such as is common to man: but God is faithful, who will not suffer you to be tempted above that ye are able; but will with the temptation also make a way to escape, that ye may be able to bear it."* When we accept Jesus' as our savior, He provides us with the armor we need to protect ourselves, *Eph 6:11-13, "Put on the whole armour of God, that ye may be able to stand against the wiles of the devil. For we wrestle not against flesh* and blood, but against principalities, against powers, against the rulers of the darkness of this world, against spiritual wickedness in high places. Wherefore take unto you the whole armour of God, that ye may be able to withstand in the evil day, and having done all, to stand."

God's armor is the Truth He gives us in His Living Word. Jesus demonstrated the power of the Truth when He spent forty days in the desert and was tempted by the devil, as our example, *Mk 1:13*, *"And he was there in the wilderness forty days, tempted of Satan; and was with the wild beasts; and the angels ministered unto him."* Every time the devil tempted Him, His answer came from the Living Word, *Matt 4:3-4, "And when the tempter came to him, he said, If thou be the Son of God, command that these stones be made bread. But he answered and said, It is written, Man shall not live by bread alone, but by every word that proceedeth out of the mouth of God."* The devil gives up when he believes we are protected by the armor of God, *Matt 4:8-11, "Again, the devil taketh him up into an exceeding high mountain, and sheweth him all the kingdoms of the world, and the glory of them; And saith unto him, All these things will I give thee, if thou wilt fall down and worship me. Then saith Jesus unto him, Get thee hence, Satan: for it is written, Thou shalt worship the Lord thy God, and him only shalt thou serve. Then the devil leaveth him, and, behold, angels came and ministered unto him."*

This is the very reason there have been so many attempts to keep the Word of God from us. Each time someone tried to eliminate or change the Word of God, God sent us someone to protect it. The Waldensians sacrificed their lives, hiding day and night in caves, in the mountains, translating the Bible by hand. The

171

Roman Catholic Church hunted them down, but God protected them so that the Living Word would reach the rest of Europe and finally bring about the Reformation. These people protected the Word of God, without changing what God had given us, *Matt 5:18*, *"For verily I say unto you, Till heaven and earth pass, one jot or one tittle shall in no wise pass from the law, till all be fulfilled."* To learn more about this part of history click this link: <u>History Of The Waldensians</u>.[48]

We cannot hide from God, or the devil, *Jer 23:24, "Who can hide in secret places so that I cannot see them?" declares the Lord. "Do not I fill heaven and earth?" declares the Lord."* So, eventually, we have to make a choice. Either we accept Jesus' invitation, or the devil will make the decision for us. There is no middle ground, *2 Cor 2:11, "Lest Satan should get an advantage of us: for we are not ignorant of his devices."*

Why is there no middle ground?

There can be no a middle ground, either we love God or we get the default decision. The devil leaves us no middle ground; he attacks us all the way along the path to God. Sort of like a huge castle under siege, those within the castle are safe, but those outside are left to the attacking forces. The devil and his followers work day and night to deceive us, *Rev 12:9, 12, "And the great dragon was cast out, that old serpent, called the Devil, and Satan, which deceiveth the whole world: he was cast out into the earth, and his angels were cast out with him. Therefore rejoice, ye heavens, and ye that dwell in them. Woe to the inhabiters of the earth and of the sea! for the devil is come down unto* you, having great wrath, because he knoweth that he hath but a short time."

God wants us all to choose Jesus, *Eze 18:32, "For I have no pleasure in the death of him that dieth, saith the Lord God: wherefore turn yourselves, and live ye."* But, He has seen the future and knows that many of us will not. So, He weeps for us, *Jn 11:35, "Jesus wept."* God's plan includes us having children, so that we might understand His weeping for His lost children. Many have accepted the default choice, to their own demise, and Cain was our first example of innocent human blood being shed, *1 Jn 3:12, "Not as Cain, who was of that wicked one, and slew his brother. And wherefore slew he him? Because his own works were evil, and his brother's righteous."* Those seeking righteousness will always be under siege from those who have not accepted Jesus. This is the battle we are in, one in which some become slaves of the devil to the point of murdering the righteous and those who might become righteous. These people have not seen they have become slaves. When they do, they begin to reason with God, for they have witnessed, first hand, the evil the devil brings.

Deut 30:19, "I call heaven and earth to record this day against you, that I have set before you life and death, blessing and cursing: therefore choose life, that both thou and thy seed may live:" God is telling us that we need to choose. Either, we will be blessed for choosing life, or not, *Eph 1:4, "According as he hath chosen us in him before the foundation of the world, that we should be holy and without blame before him in love:"* He has chosen to invite all of us, knowing many will not accept His invitation, *1 Tim 2:3-6, "For this is good and acceptable in the sight of God our Saviour; Who will have all men to be saved, and to come unto the knowledge of the truth. For there is one God, and one mediator between God and men, the man Christ Jesus; Who gave himself a ransom for all, to be testified in due time."* He only asks us to reason with Him before we are captured by the devil, *Is 1:18, "Come now, and let us reason together, saith the Lord: though your sins be as scarlet, they shall be as white as snow; though they be red like crimson, they shall be as wool."* God is knocking at the door of our hearts, asking us to open that door for Him to enter, *Rev 3:20, "Behold, I stand at the door, and knock: if any man hear my voice, and open the door, I will come in to him, and will sup with him, and he with me."* The vision this provides is one of a loving father, knocking at the door of His child's heart, hoping the child will accept the father's love and friendship. It can be a joyful vision, or a sad one of lost hopes and love.

Once we open the door, He will respond by opening the castle doors, allowing us to enter into the safety of His protection and love. It is comforting to know that no matter who we are, or what we have done, God is always ready to forgive us, always ready to become our friend and adopt us into His eternal family, *1 Jn 1:9, "If we confess our sins, he is faithful and just to forgive us our sins, and to cleanse us from all unrighteousness."* This is how we accept His invitation to enter His castle; we confess our sins, even though God already knows them. Sort of like letting go of the rings on the jungle gyms so that we can fall to the safety of solid ground. At first we are afraid to let go, but when we do our fear dissipates as we safely land on His solid ground, *Jam 5:16, "Confess your faults one to another, and pray one for another, that ye may be healed. The effectual fervent prayer of a righteous man availeth much."* Confessing our sins to one another is letting go of them. This process allows not only the sinner to let go, but also anyone who was negatively affected by the sin, for this gives them the opportunity to forgive, *Lk 17:3, "Take heed to yourselves: If thy brother trespass against thee, rebuke him; and if he repent, forgive him."* Everyone is healed and this process removes the roadblocks from the path that leads to God's love.

God wants us to know who the devil is, so that we might seek God's protection before it is too late, *Jn 8:44, "Ye are of your father the devil, and the lusts of your father ye will do. He was a murderer from the beginning, and abode not in the truth, because there is no truth in him. When he speaketh a lie, he speaketh of his own: for he is a liar, and the father of it."* When we refuse to reason with God we have made the decision to wander on the outside of the castle, lost in the fog of our own ways and devices, *Prov 1:29-31, "For that they hated knowledge, and did not choose the fear of the Lord: They would none of my counsel: they despised all my reproof. Therefore shall they eat of the fruit of their own way, and be filled with their own devices."* So, there is a choice to be made and when we do not choose to reason with God, we have chosen the default decision of dealing with the devil on our own. *Prov 14:12, "There is a way which seemeth right unto a man, but the end thereof are the ways of death."*

Josh 24:15, "And if it seem evil unto you to serve the Lord, choose you this day whom ye will serve; whether the gods which your fathers served

175

that were on the other side of the flood, or the gods of the Amorites, in whose land ye dwell: but as for me and my house, we will serve the Lord." Joshua is saying he made a decision and he is challenging everyone else to make one. He finds it difficult to understand why anyone who was with him would hesitate, considering all they had seen God do. He knows that if we honestly consider the choices and then make a decision, we will choose God.

When we reason with God, it becomes ever more clear, that the purpose we are called to is the one He created. Each day we reason with Him the best path for our lives becomes easier to see, as the fog of the lies of this world dissipate. There was no fog left between Joshua and God, which is why it was so easy for him to make the decision.

Middle ground is an illusion created by the devil. There is no middle ground, we must choose!

So, who are we? We are God's created beings with a decision to make!

Who is Jesus?

"Who is Jesus?"

Jn 1:1, "In the beginning was the Word, and the Word was with God, and the Word was God." John reported it, so he must have believed it.

Rev 1:13, 17, "And in the midst of the seven candlesticks one like unto the Son of man, clothed with a garment down to the foot, and girt about the paps with a golden girdle...And when I saw him, I fell at his feet as dead. And he laid his right hand upon me, saying unto me, Fear not; I am the first and the last:" John reported it near the end of his life, so he still believed it.

Matt 16:16-17, "And Simon Peter answered and said, Thou art the Christ, the Son of the living God. And Jesus answered and said unto him, Blessed art thou, Simon Barjona: for flesh and blood hath not revealed it unto thee, but my Father which is in heaven." Apparently, Peter believed it and Matthew reported it, so he must have believed he heard it.

Mk 8:29-30, "And he saith unto them, But whom say ye that I am? And Peter answereth and saith unto him, Thou art the Christ. And he charged them that they should tell no man of him." Peter thought Jesus was the Son of God and Mark reported it, so he must have believed he heard it.

Tit 2:13, "Looking for that blessed hope, and the glorious appearing of the great God and our Saviour Jesus Christ;" Paul thought Jesus was the Son of God.

Lk 9:20-23, "He said unto them, But whom say ye that I am? Peter answering said, The Christ of God. And he straitly charged them, and commanded them to tell no man that thing; Saying, The Son of man must suffer many things, and be rejected of the elders and chief priests and scribes, and be slain, and be raised the third day. And he said to them all, If any man will come after me, let him deny himself, and take up his cross daily, and follow me." Luke reported it, so he must have believed he heard it.

Mk 14:61-63, "But he held his peace, and answered nothing. Again the high priest asked him, and said unto him, Art thou the Christ, the Son of the Blessed? And Jesus said, I am: and ye shall see the Son of man sitting on the right hand of power, and coming in the clouds of heaven. Then the high priest rent his clothes, and saith, What need we any further witnesses?" Jesus is using the same name used by Daniel, *Dan 7:13-14, "I saw in the night visions, and, behold, one like the Son of man came with the clouds of heaven, and came to the Ancient of days, and they brought him near before him. And there was given him dominion, and glory, and a kingdom, that all people, nations, and languages, should serve him: his dominion is an everlasting dominion, which shall not pass away, and his kingdom that which shall not be destroyed."*

Jn 5:17-18, "But Jesus answered them, My Father worketh hitherto, and I work. Therefore the Jews sought the more to kill him, because he not only had broken the sabbath, but said also that God was his Father, making himself equal with God." The Jews understood that Jesus was claiming to be the Son of God.

Jn 6:38, 40, 64-70, "For I have come down from heaven not to do my will but to do the will of him who sent me...And this is the will of him that sent me, that every one which seeth the Son, and believeth on him, may have everlasting life: and I will raise him up at the last day...But there are some of you that believe not. For Jesus knew from the beginning who they were that believed not, and who should betray him. And he said, Therefore said I unto you, that no man can come unto me, except it were given unto him of my Father. From that time many of his disciples went back, and walked no more with him. Then said Jesus unto the twelve, Will ye also go away? Then Simon Peter answered him, Lord, to whom shall we go? thou hast the words of eternal life. And we believe and are sure that thou art that Christ, the Son of the living God. Jesus answered them, Have not I chosen you twelve, and one of you is a devil?"* Jesus tells us that He came down from heaven to do His Father's will.

Jn 8:56-58, "Your father Abraham rejoiced to see my day: and he saw it, and was glad. Then said the Jews unto him, Thou art not yet fifty years old, and hast thou seen Abraham? Jesus said unto them, Verily, verily, I say unto you, Before Abraham was, I am." Jesus is using the very words used by God when He spoke to Moses, *Ex 3:14, "And God said unto Moses, I Am That I Am: and he said, Thus shalt thou say unto the children of Israel, I Am hath sent me unto you."*

Jn 10:30, 36, "I and my Father are one... Say ye of him, whom the Father hath sanctified, and sent into the world, Thou blasphemest; because I said, I am the Son of God?" Jesus confirms His claim to be the Son of God.

Jn 11:43, "And when he thus had spoken, he cried with a loud voice, Lazarus, come forth. And he that was dead came forth, bound hand and foot with graveclothes: and his face was bound about with a napkin. Jesus saith unto them, Loose him, and let him go." Only God can resurrect the dead.

Lk 5:20-21, "And when he saw their faith, he said unto him, Man, thy sins are forgiven thee. And the scribes and the Pharisees began to reason, saying, Who is this which speaketh blasphemies? Who can forgive sins, but God alone?" The Pharisees knew that no one but God can forgive sins, but Jesus did it many times.

Jn 10:25, "Jesus answered them, I told you, and ye believed not: the works that I do in my Father's name, they bear witness of me." The Jews who heard this knew He was claiming to be the Son of God and that the miracles they had witnessed were to be the evidence they were to believe, since they did not believe Him when He told them.

Phil 2:6, "Who, being in the form of God, thought it not robbery to be equal with God:" Paul understands the importance of Jesus claim of being equal with God.

Mk 4:39, "And he arose, and rebuked the wind, and said unto the sea, Peace, be still. And the wind ceased, and there was a great calm." Who but God can tell the sea to be calm? Mark witnessed it and reports it.

Jn 20:28, "And Thomas answered and said unto him, My Lord and my God. Jesus saith unto him, Thomas, because thou hast seen me, thou hast believed: blessed are they that have not seen, and yet have believed." It was easy for Thomas to believe, he was able to put his hand into the wound on Jesus' side, but Jesus is telling us those who believe on faith alone will be blessed. It is clear that Thomas believed Jesus is the Son of God. *Rev 19:9, "And he saith unto me, Write, Blessed are they* which are called unto the marriage supper of the Lamb. And he saith unto me, These are the true sayings of God." The blessed will come to the wedding party because they believed without seeing.

Jn 8:46, "Which of you convinceth me of sin? And if I say the truth, why do ye not believe me?" and 2 Cor 5:21, *"For he hath made him to be sin for us, who knew no sin; that we might be made the righteousness of God in him."* and 1 Jn 3:5, *"And ye know that he was manifested to take away our sins; and in him is no sin."* and 1 Pet 2:22, *"Who did no sin, neither was guile found in his mouth:"* Jesus tells us He did not sin, Paul, John and Peter tell us He did not sin. These people went on to give up their lives, not as terrorists but as martyrs for their belief Jesus is the Son of God. Peter tells us Jesus never sinned.

Matt 11:2-5, "Now when John had heard in the prison the works of Christ, he sent two of his disciples, And said unto him, Art thou he that should come, or do we look for another? Jesus answered and said unto them, Go and shew John again those things which ye do hear and see: The blind receive their sight, and the lame walk, the lepers are cleansed, and the deaf hear, the dead are raised up, and the poor have the gospel preached to them." Jesus is not only comforting John with this statement, He is telling us that we can believe He is God.

Jn 17:5, "And now, O Father, glorify thou me with thine own self with the glory which I had with thee before the world was." Jesus tells us that He had the glory of God before the world was created.

These are but a few of the verses where Jesus made it perfectly clear, for all who are willing to listen; He is the Son of God. He is God. He and the Father are one. He told us He is the only way, the

Truth, and the life, *Jn 14:6, "Jesus saith unto him, I am the way, the truth, and the life: no man cometh unto the Father, but by me."*

So, are Christians arrogant in believing that Jesus is the only way to God? Is that not being narrow minded? The truth is narrow; anything less than the truth is some version of a lie, sometimes close to the truth and sometimes very far from it. Jesus, who is God, claimed He is the only way to God. Christians are merely repeating the truth Jesus proclaimed about Himself. We may not like hearing the Truth, but if it is the Truth, it does not matter whether we like hearing it, or not. Either, we believe Jesus is the Son of God, or not, each of us will have to make our own decision. There are many who kill the messengers of Truth, for no other reason than they are telling the Truth. Is this not yet another proof that Jesus is the Son of God? He did not tell us to kill those who do not believe, He told us to love them, to forgive them, and to pray for them. Are we paying attention to the fruits?

Finally, the proof of Christ's deity can be seen today in the lives of countless men, women, and children. Each day, people of every tongue, tribe and nation experience the resurrected Christ by repenting of their sins and receiving Jesus as their Lord and Savior. The lives they lead after receiving Jesus as their savior testify to His existence, *Matt 7:16, "Ye shall know them by their fruits. Do men gather grapes of thorns, or figs of thistles?"* For those of us who are not yet Christians, it might be time to look closely for the fruits of the lives of those who are truly following God's Word. There is no stronger evidence! Jesus is the Son of God!

The Bible makes it clear that Jesus thinks He is the Son of God, the apostles thought He was the Son of God, but many today still will not even consider the possibility that He really lived. To help the skeptic find the Truth we will examine several different sources, found outside of the Bible.

Our first source will be the writings of Flavius Josephus, a first century Jewish Historian. Josephus wrote a twenty volume historical work on the history of the Jewish people entitled "Antiquities of the Jews", here is the link: <u>Antiquities Of The Jews.</u>[49] Jesus is referred to twice in this work, volumes 18 and 20. Josephus was not a Christian and did not believe Jesus was the Messiah spoken of in the Old Testament. However, his mentioning of Jesus and Jesus' brother James says he believed there really was a Jesus and that He was really crucified by Pilate. His detailed account of the arrest and beheading of John the Baptist is further proof of the accuracy of the Biblical accounts regarding John. In volume 18 Josephus describes the sentencing and crucifixion of Jesus at the hands of Roman authorities, here is the link: <u>Josephus On Jesus.</u>[50]

Our second source is Cornelius Tacitus, a Roman Senator and one of the greatest Roman historians. Tactitus mentions Jesus in his final work "The Annals", here is the link: <u>The Annals</u>[51], covering the period from the death of Augustus Caesar in 14 AD to Nero's death in 68 AD. The Annals is one of the earliest secular historical records to mention Christ, which Tacitus does in connection with Nero's persecution of the Christians, here are the links: <u>Nero's Persecution Of The Christians</u>[52] and <u>The Annuals, Book 14 Chapter 44.</u>[53] Tacitus tells of the extreme penalty Christ pays at the hands of Pontius Pilatus.

Our third source is Gaius Plinius Caecilius Secundus, better known as Pliny the Younger, here is the link: Pliny The Younger[54], who was a lawyer, author, and magistrate of Ancient Rome. According to Wikipedia: "Pliny is known for his hundreds of surviving letters, which are an invaluable historical source for the time period. Many are addressed to reigning emperors or to notables such as the historian, Tacitus. Pliny himself was a notable figure, serving as an imperial magistrate under Trajan (reigned AD 98–117). Pliny was considered an honest and moderate man, consistent in his pursuit of suspected Christian members according to Roman law, and rose through a series of Imperial civil and military offices, the cursus honorum."

In a letter to emperor Trajan, Pliny the Younger wrote, "They were accustomed to meet on a fixed day before dawn and sing responsively a hymn to Christ as to a god, and bound themselves to a solemn oath, not to any wicked deeds, but never to commit any fraud, theft, adultery, never to falsify their word, not to deny a trust when they should be called upon to deliver it up. When this was over, it was their custom to depart and to assemble again to partake of a meal–but ordinary and innocent food." Here is a link: Pliny The Younger On Christians.[55] Pliny goes on to say that under penalty of death, the Christians he met would not disavow Christ as their savior and the Son of God.

Our fourth source is Sextus Julius Africanus a Christian traveler and historian of the late 2nd and early 3rd century AD. He wrote "Chronographiai", a five-book history of the world from creation to 221 AD. "An eclipse of the sun'unreasonably, as it seems to me (unreasonably of course, because a solar eclipse could not take place at the time of the full moon, and it was at the season of the Paschal full moon that Christ died." Julius Africanus, Chronography, 18. The importance of this quote is two fold as it shows: 1) proof of Jesus' existence and 2) yet another confirmation of the Bible's account of Jesus' crucifixion. Matthew tells us about the period of darkness in, *Matt 27:45, "Now from the sixth hour there was darkness over all the land unto the ninth hour."* The "sixth hour" is noon and the ninth hour is 3:00 PM, here is the link: Sextus Julius Africanus.[56] Africanus quotes the historian Thallus, our fifth source: Thallus[57], who was trying to explain the odd occurrence of the sky being dark at noon during the crucifxion of Jesus as an eclipse. Africanus also quotes the secular scholar Phlegon, our sixth source, here is a link: Phlegon[58], a Greek Historian who lived in the 2nd century AD and also wrote of an eclipse occurring on the day Jesus was crucified.

Our seventh source is Lucian of Samosate, a well-known Greek satirist and traveling lecturer who mocked Christians in his writings, and at the same time provided evidence that Jesus really did exist: "He was second only to that one whom they still worship today, the man in Palestine who was crucified because he brought this new form of initiation into the world." "Having convinced themselves that they are immortal and will live forever, the poor wretches despise death and most willingly give themselves to it. Moreover, that first lawgiver of theirs persuaded them that they are all brothers the moment they transgress and deny the Greek gods and begin worshiping that crucified sophist and living by his laws." "They scorn all possessions without distinction and treat them as community property. They accept such things on faith alone, without any evidence. So if a fraudulent and cunning person who knows how to take advantage of a situation comes among them, he can make himself rich in a short time." Even though Lucian does not mention Jesus by name, there is no doubt he is speaking of Jesus as he confirms: 1) that he was crucified in "Palestine" (the name of Israel at that time), 2) had followers who believed in eternal life, 3) that they were all equal in Christ, and that Christians deny all other gods and believe on "faith alone." The Bible's clear statements about the Christian faith validate this evidence from outside of the Bible that Jesus the "man in Palestine" did exist. Link for more on: Lucian.[59]

Our eighth source is Gaius Suetonius Tranquillus, commonly known as Suetonius, who was a Roman historian belonging to the equestrian order in the early Imperial era. His most important surviving work is a set of biographies of twelve successive Roman rulers, from Julius Caesar to Domitian, entitled "De Vita Caesarum". In his writings he reports that the emperor expelled the Jews from Rome, since they "constantly made disturbances at the instigation of Christ." Here is the link for source information on Suetonius: The Twelve Caesars.[60]

Even with these proofs from other sources, the Bible still remains the best historical evidence that Jesus existed. No other surviving historical manuscript has more verifiable copies still in existence today. The Old Testament prophesized the coming of the Messiah, some of these prophecies were written over a thousand years before His birth, here is a link: <u>Prophecies Jesus Fulfilled</u>.[61] The New Testament documents Jesus' fulfillment of all of the Old Testament prophecies written about Him.

Bible skeptics, atheists and those who like to challenge Christianity say, when discussing the historical aspects of the Bible, "you cannot use the Bible as proof that Jesus existed. You must use non-Bible sources!!" Wrong! The normal objective measure of the reliability of historical documents is: 1) The number of available copies of the ancient manuscript and 2) the time span between the original version and the date of those copies still in existence today. When examined under this standard, the Bible proves to be more reliable than any other historical manuscript.

Here are links to some of the earliest manuscript fragments of the New Testament: <u>John Rylands Fragment</u>[62], <u>Chester Beatty Papyrus</u>[63] and the <u>Bodmer Papyrus</u>[64], which were written between 50-100AD. Copies of these papyri were reproduced in 125-200AD, meaning that the time span between the originals and the copies still in existence today is 25 years to 150 years, putting all these manuscripts written anywhere from 17-167 years after the death of Jesus Christ. We can object to this time span, however, it is shorter than almost any other document proving the existence of any other historical figure.

The Bible has more verifiable historical evidence that validates the existence of Jesus, than exists for Plato, Aristotle, or Homer. Here is a link: Evidence Of Christ's Existence.[65]

Let us explore the Bible to see if we might find proof that Jesus does exist. The Bible says God gave us prophecies and then fulfilled them, so we would be able find our way to Him, *Is 46:9-10*, *"Remember the former things of old: for I am God, and there is none else; I am God, and there is none like me, Declaring the end from the beginning, and from ancient times the things that are not yet done, saying, My counsel shall stand, and I will do all my pleasure:"* God is not going to force us to come to Him, He allows us to find Him in His Living Word. Here are the prophecies fulfilled from His Living Word:

1 - Written in 2067 BC - *Gen 17:19, "And God said, Sarah thy wife shall bear thee a son indeed; and thou shalt call his name Isaac: and I will establish my covenant with him for an everlasting covenant, and with his seed after him."* Abraham and Isaac are in the bloodline that leads to the seed that will bring the everlasting covenant, Jesus. *Lk 3:34, "Which was the son of Jacob, which was the son of Isaac, which was the son of Abraham, which was the son of Thara, which was the son of Nachor,"* God has given us Jesus bloodline to further demonstrate the fulfillment of the prophecies made centuries earlier.

2 - Written in 1859 BC - *Gen 49:10, "The sceptre shall not depart from Judah, nor a lawgiver from between his feet, until Shiloh come; and unto him shall the gathering of the people be."* Jesus would come from

the tribe of Judah. *Heb 7:14, "For it is evident that our Lord sprang out of Juda; of which tribe Moses spake nothing concerning priesthood."*

3 - Written in 979 BC - *Ps 2:6, "Yet have I set my king upon my holy hill of Zion."* Jesus would be called king. *Matt 27:37, "And set up over his head his accusation written, This Is Jesus The King Of The Jews."*

4 - Written in 979 BC - *Ps 2:7, "I will declare the decree: the Lord hath said unto me, Thou art my Son; this day have I begotten thee."* Jesus would be called the Son of God. *Matt 3:16-17, "And Jesus, when he was baptized, went up straightway out of the water: and, lo, the heavens were opened unto him, and he saw the Spirit of God descending like a dove, and lighting upon him: And lo a voice from heaven, saying, This is my beloved Son, in whom I am well pleased."*

5 - Written in 979 BC - *Ps 16:10-11, "For thou wilt not leave my soul in hell; neither wilt thou suffer thine Holy One to see corruption. Thou wilt shew me the path of life: in thy presence is fulness of joy; at thy right hand there are pleasures for evermore."* Jesus would be resurrected. *Matt 28:2-7, "And, behold, there was a great earthquake: for the angel of the Lord descended from heaven, and came and rolled back the stone from the door, and sat upon it. His countenance was like lightning, and his raiment white as snow: And for fear of him the keepers did shake, and became as dead men. And the angel answered and said unto the women, Fear not ye: for I know that ye seek Jesus, which was crucified. He is not here: for he is risen, as he said. Come, see the place where the Lord lay. And go quickly, and tell his disciples that he is risen from the dead; and, behold, he goeth before you into Galilee; there shall ye see him: lo, I have told you."*

6 - Written in 979 BC - *Ps 22:1, "My God, my God, why hast thou forsaken me? why art thou so far from helping me, and from the words of my roaring?"* There would be a moment when Jesus feels forsaken by God. *Matt 27:46, "And about the ninth hour Jesus cried with a loud voice, saying, Eli, Eli, lama sabachthani? that is to say, My God, my God, why hast thou forsaken me?"*

7 - Written in 979 BC - *Ps 22:7-8, "All they that see me laugh me to scorn: they shoot out the lip, they shake the head, saying, He trusted on the Lord that he would deliver him: let him deliver him, seeing he delighted in him."* Jesus would be mocked and scorned. *Lk 23:35, "And the people stood beholding. And the rulers also with them derided him, saying, He saved others; let him save himself, if he be Christ, the chosen of God."*

8 - Written in 979 BC - *Ps 22:16, "For dogs have compassed me: the assembly of the wicked have inclosed me: they pierced my hands and my feet."* Jesus would have His hands and feet pierced. *Jn 20:25-27, "The other disciples therefore said unto him, We have seen the Lord. But he said unto them, Except I shall see in his hands the print of the nails, and put my finger into the print of the nails, and thrust my hand into his side, I will not believe. And after eight days again his disciples were within, and Thomas with them: then came Jesus, the doors being shut, and stood in the midst, and said, Peace be unto you. Then saith he to Thomas, Reach hither thy finger, and behold my hands; and reach hither thy hand, and thrust it into my side: and be not faithless, but believing."* There are many Thomas' in our world today, but no resurrected Jesus for them to put their hands into. We need to accept that Thomas already

satisfied our skepticism by putting his hand into Jesus side and then having it documented in the Gospels.

9 - Written in 979 BC - *Ps 22:18, "They part my garments among them, and cast lots upon my vesture."* They would gamble for Jesus' clothing. *Lk 23:34, "Then said Jesus, Father, forgive them; for they know not what they do. And they parted his raiment, and cast lots."* No wonder the skeptics refuse to read the Bible, for the Bible is loaded with proofs of Jesus' existence and many of us are too afraid to learn the Truth. However, putting our head in the sand has never proved to be an effective way to deal with the Truth. Every time someone tells me they refuse to read the Bible, I get a profound sense of sadness, for I know it will be more difficult for them to find their way to God.

10 - Written in 979 BC - *Ps 35:11, "False witnesses did rise up; they laid to my charge things that I knew not."* People would falsely testify against Jesus. *Mk 14:57-59, "And there arose certain, and bare false witness against him, saying, We heard him say, I will destroy this temple that is made with hands, and within three days I will build another made without hands. But neither so did their witness agree together."*

11 - Written in 979 BC - *Ps 35:19, "Let not them that are mine enemies wrongfully rejoice over me: neither let them wink with the eye that hate me without a cause."* Jesus would be hated without cause. *Jn 15:24-25, "If I had not done among them the works which none other man did, they had not had sin: but now have they both seen and hated both me and my Father. But this cometh to pass, that the word might be fulfilled that is written in their law, They hated me without a cause."* Jesus knew

He was to fulfill all of the prophecies the Old Testament made regarding Him. He also knew that people would hate Him for bringing the Truth. The sad thing is that people still hate Him today, without a cause! He asked us to love Him and our neighbor, and people hate Him for it?

12 - Written in 979 BC - *Ps 41:9, "Yea, mine own familiar friend, in whom I trusted, which did eat of my bread, hath lifted up his heel against me."* A friend would betray Jesus. *Lk 22:47-48, "And while he yet spake, behold a multitude, and he that was called Judas, one of the twelve, went before them, and drew near unto Jesus to kiss him. But Jesus said unto him, Judas, betrayest thou the Son of man with a kiss?"* Betrayed with a kiss, only a friend would use this method of identifying Jesus.

13 - Written in 979 BC - *Ps 69:21, "They gave me also gall for my meat; and in my thirst they gave me vinegar to drink."* Jesus would be given vinegar to drink. *Matt 27:34, "They gave him vinegar to drink mingled with gall: and when he had tasted thereof, he would not drink."*

14 - Written in 979 BC - *Ps 78:2-4, "I will open my mouth in a parable: I will utter dark sayings of old: Which we have heard and known, and our fathers have told us. We will not hide them from their children, shewing to the generation to come the praises of the Lord, and his strength, and his wonderful works that he hath done."* Jesus would speak in parables. *Matt 13:10, "And the disciples came, and said unto him, Why speakest thou unto them in parables?"*

15 - Written in 979 BC - *Ps 109:4-5, "For my love they are my adversaries: but I give myself unto prayer. And they have rewarded me evil*

for good, and hatred for my love." Jesus would pray for His enemies. *Lk 23:34, "Then said Jesus, Father, forgive them; for they know not what they do. And they parted his raiment, and cast lots."* Not only did He pray for them, He gave us further proof in that many will repay His love with hatred. For those that think this is too strong a statement, today's proof is fully demonstrated in the voices and faces of those that are trying to remove all traces of God from our country.

16 - Written in 735 BC - *Is 7:14, "Therefore the Lord himself shall give you a sign; Behold, a virgin shall conceive, and bear a son, and shall call his name Immanuel."* Jesus would be born of a virgin. *Matt 1:23, "Behold, a virgin shall be with child, and shall bring forth a son, and they shall call his name Emmanuel, which being interpreted is, God with us."* and *Lk 1:26-27, 35, 1:11, "And in the sixth month the angel Gabriel was sent from God unto a city of Galilee, named Nazareth, To a virgin espoused to a man whose name was Joseph, of the house of David; and the virgin's name was Mary....And the angel answered and said unto her, The Holy Ghost shall come upon thee, and the power of the Highest shall overshadow thee: therefore also that holy thing which shall be born of thee shall be called the Son of God....For unto you is born this day in the city of David a Saviour, which is Christ the Lord."*

17 - Written in 735 BC - *Micah 5:2, "But thou, Bethlehem Ephratah, though thou be little among the thousands of Judah, yet out of thee shall he come forth unto me that is to be ruler in Israel; whose goings forth have been from of old, from everlasting."* Jesus would be born in Bethlehem. *Matt 2:1, "Now when Jesus was born in Bethlehem of Judaea in the days of Herod the king, behold, there came wise men from the east to Jerusalem,"*

18 - Written in 730 BC - *Is 11:1, "And there shall come forth a rod out of the stem of Jesse, and a Branch shall grow out of his roots:"* Jesus' bloodline comes through Jesse. *Matt 1:5, "And Salmon begat Booz of Rachab; and Booz begat Obed of Ruth; and Obed begat Jesse;"* This is just another example of why God gave us the complete bloodline of Jesus.

19 - Written in 711 BC - *Is 40:3, "The voice of him that crieth in the wilderness, Prepare ye the way of the Lord, make straight in the desert a highway for our God."* A messenger would come to prepare the way for Jesus. *Lk 3:2-3, "Annas and Caiaphas being the high priests, the word of God came unto John the son of Zacharias in the wilderness. And he came into all the country about Jordan, preaching the baptism of repentance for the remission of sins;"* It was John the Baptist who wandered the country preaching, baptizing and preparing the way for our Lord Jesus, whom he also baptized.

20 - Written in 711 BC - *Is 50:6, "I gave my back to the smiters, and my cheeks to them that plucked off the hair: I hid not my face from shame and spitting."* Jesus would be hit and spit upon. *Matt 26:67, "Then did they spit in his face, and buffeted him; and others smote him with the palms of their hands,"* My heart aches when I read this passage. Watching the movie "The Passion of Christ" is very difficult for this very same reason!

21 - Written in 711 BC - *Is 53:5-6, "But he was wounded for our transgressions, he was bruised for our iniquities: the chastisement of our peace was upon him; and with his stripes we are healed. All we like sheep have gone astray; we have turned every one to his own way; and the Lord*

hath laid on him the iniquity of us all." Jesus would have all of our sins placed upon Him. *1 Cor 15:3, "For I delivered unto you first of all that which I also received, how that Christ died for our sins according to the scriptures;"*

22 - Written in 711 BC - *Is 53:7, "He was oppressed, and he was afflicted, yet he opened not his mouth: he is brought as a lamb to the slaughter, and as a sheep before her shearers is dumb, so he openeth not his mouth."* Jesus would not open His mouth to defend Himself. *Mk 15:4-5, "And Pilate asked him again, saying, Answerest thou nothing? behold how many things they witness against thee. But Jesus yet answered nothing; so that Pilate marvelled."*

23 - Written in 711 BC - *Is 53:9, "And he made his grave with the wicked, and with the rich in his death; because he had done no violence, neither was any deceit in his mouth."* Jesus would die in the presence of the wicked and buried with the rich. *Matt 27:38, "Then were there two thieves crucified with him, one on the right hand, and another on the left."* and *Matt 27:57-60, "When the even was come, there came a rich man of Arimathaea, named Joseph, who also himself was Jesus' disciple: He went to Pilate, and begged the body of Jesus. Then Pilate commanded the body to be delivered. And when Joseph had taken the body, he wrapped it in a clean linen cloth, And laid it in his own new tomb, which he had hewn out in the rock: and he rolled a great stone to the door of the sepulchre, and departed."*

24 - Written in 520 BC - *Zech 11:13, "And the Lord said unto me, Cast it unto the potter: a goodly price that I was prised at of them. And I took the thirty pieces of silver, and cast them to the potter in the house of*

the Lord." The thirty pieces of silver would be given for the betrayal of Jesus. *Matt 27:9, "Then was fulfilled that which was spoken by Jeremy the prophet, saying, And they took the thirty pieces of silver, the price of him that was valued, whom they of the children of Israel did value;"*

We have seen 24 of the more than 300 prophecies Jesus fulfilled. Here is a link for a more complete study of them: 365 Prophecies Jesus Fulfilled.[66]

All the prophets told us the Messiah would come to offer us salvation. *Acts 10:43, "To Him give all the prophets witness, that through His name whosoever believeth in Him shall receive remission of sins."* Jesus is that Messiah!

This world needs the hope Jesus has brought us. The fact that people still commit suicide today testifies to the lack of hope in this world. Be assured, there will be no suicides in Heaven. Jesus provides that needed hope for those who come to believe in Him, *Tit 2:13, "Looking for that blessed hope, and the glorious appearing of the great God and our Saviour Jesus Christ;"*

Rev 21:4, "And God shall wipe away all tears from their eyes; and there shall be no more death, neither sorrow, nor crying, neither shall there be any more pain: for the former things are passed away." What a wonderful hope we have in Jesus!

Who is Jesus? The Son of the Living God sent to die for our sins and to offer us eternity, *Gal 1:4, "Who gave himself for our sins, that he might deliver us from this present evil world, according to the will of God and our Father:"*

Why Did Jesus Come?

Jesus came:

1 - To do the will of God the Father, *Jn 4:34, "Jesus saith unto them, My meat is to do the will of him that sent me, and to finish his work."* and *Heb 10:7 "Then said I, Lo, I come (in the volume of the book it is written of me,) to do thy will, O God.",* so that we might learn from His example, *Matt 12:50, "For whosoever shall do the will of my Father which is in heaven, the same is my brother, and sister, and mother."* Abram followed the will of God, most of the time, *Gen 12:1, "Now the Lord had said unto Abram, Get thee out of thy country, and from thy kindred, and from thy father's house, unto a land that I will shew thee:"* Jesus followed the will of God all of the time.

2 - To bring us the sword of Truth, *Jn 18:37, "Pilate therefore said unto him, Art thou a king then? Jesus answered, Thou sayest that I am a king. To this end was I born, and for this cause came I into the world, that I should bear witness unto the truth. Every one that is of the truth heareth my voice."* Jesus is telling us that He was born to bring us the Truth, and the truth is He is the King of Kings. If we do not understand this, we will not understand the message of the Bible. This is why false teachers abound, attempting to lead us away from the Truth. We cannot let these false teachers keep us from the sword of Truth Jesus brought, *Matt 10:34-36, "Think not that I am come to send peace on earth: I came not to send peace, but a sword. For I am come to set a man at variance against his father, and the daughter against her mother, and the*

daughter in law against her mother in law. And a man's foes shall be they of his own household." Jesus is preparing us, for once we accept Him, as our savior we will have foes; and sadly some of them will be within our own families.

Mk 1:38, "And he said unto them, Let us go into the next towns, that I may preach there also: for therefore came I forth." People needed to hear the Truth directly from Jesus, so that His testimony could not be challenged after His death. This is why we find no documented historical evidence that refutes the Apostles message. Too many people had heard the Truth with their own ears, had seen Jesus heal the sick, raise the dead, walk on water, and eat with sinners, *Acts 1:9-11, "And when he had spoken these things, while they beheld, he was taken up; and a cloud received him out of their sight. And while they looked stedfastly toward heaven as he went up, behold, two men stood by them in white apparel; Which also said, Ye men of Galilee, why stand ye gazing up into heaven? this same Jesus, which is taken up from you into heaven, shall so come in like manner as ye have seen him go into heaven."* Jesus left no room for false evidence about the Apostles' message, He allowed the men of Galilee to witness His ascension with their own eyes. He brought with Him the whole armor of God to protect us from the devil, *Eph 6:11, "Put on the whole armour of God, that ye may be able to stand against the wiles of the devil."*

3 - To show us the Father, *Jn 14:9, "Jesus saith unto him, Have I been so long time with you, and yet hast thou not known me, Philip? he that hath seen me hath seen the Father; and how sayest thou then, Show us the Father?"* and *Matt 11:27, "All things are delivered unto me of my*

Father: and no man knoweth the Son, but the Father; neither knoweth any man the Father, save the Son, and he to whomsoever the Son will reveal him." Jesus wants all of us to know the Father, for when we are armed with this Truth, no one will be able to steal our salvation, 2 Jn 1-10, *"The elder unto the elect lady and her children, whom I love in the truth; and not I only, but also all they that have known the truth; For the truth's sake, which dwelleth in us, and shall be with us for ever. Grace be with you, mercy, and peace, from God the Father, and from the Lord Jesus Christ, the Son of the Father, in truth and love. I rejoiced greatly that I found of thy children walking in truth, as we have received a commandment from the Father. And now I beseech thee, lady, not as though I wrote a new commandment unto thee, but that which we had from the beginning, that we love one another. And this is love, that we walk after his commandments. This is the commandment, That, as ye have heard from the beginning, ye should walk in it. For many deceivers are entered into the world, who confess not that Jesus Christ is come in the flesh. This is a deceiver and an antichrist. Look to yourselves, that we lose not those things which we have wrought, but that we receive a full reward. Whosoever transgresseth, and abideth not in the doctrine of Christ, hath not God. He that abideth in the doctrine of Christ, he hath both the Father and the Son. If there come any unto you, and bring not this doctrine, receive him not into your house, neither bid him God speed:"*

4 - To save the lost with His light, Lk 19:10, *"For the Son of man is come to seek and to save that which was lost."* and Lk 4:43, *"And he said unto them, I must preach the kingdom of God to other cities also: for therefore am I sent."* and 1 Tim 1:15, *"This is a faithful saying, and worthy of all acceptation, that Christ Jesus came into the world to save*

sinners; of whom I am chief." and *Matt 18:11, "For the Son of man is come to save that which was lost."* and *Acts 4:12, "Salvation is found in no one else, for there is no other name under heaven given to mankind by which we must be saved."* and *Phil 3:20, "But our citizenship is in heaven. And we eagerly await a Savior from there, the Lord Jesus Christ,"* and *Matt 9:13, "But go ye and learn what that meaneth, I will have mercy, and not sacrifice: for I am not come to call the righteous, but sinners to repentance."* and *Lk 9:56, "For the Son of man is not come to destroy men's lives, but to save them. And they went to another village."* and *Jn 3:17, "For God sent not his Son into the world to condemn the world; but that the world through him might be saved."* and *1 Jn 4:9, "In this was manifested the love of God toward us, because that God sent his only begotten Son into the world, that we might live through him."* When we see His light and repent from our sins, we are saved. We are all sinners, however, once we accept His grace, we begin the journey of removing sin from our lives, *2 Tim 3:16-17, "All scripture is given by inspiration of God, and is profitable for doctrine, for reproof, for correction, for instruction in righteousness: That the man of God may be perfect, thoroughly furnished unto all good works."* This transformation process allows Jesus to present us to the Father, white as snow, *Is 1:18, "Come now, and let us reason together, saith the Lord: though your sins be as scarlet, they shall be as white as snow; though they be red like crimson, they shall be as wool."*

Jn 12:46-47, "I am come a light into the world, that whosoever believeth on me should not abide in darkness. And if any man hear my words, and believe not, I judge him not: for I came not to judge the world, but to save the world." Jesus is the light that has come into this dark world, to light our path, *Ps 119:105, "Thy word is a lamp unto my feet, and a light unto my path."*

His light leads us to accept Jesus as our savior, the only mediator there is between God and man, *1 Tim 2:5, "For there is one God, and one mediator between God and men, the man Christ Jesus;"*

5 - To be our example, to love and to serve, *Mk 10:45, "For even the Son of man came not to be ministered unto, but to minister, and to give his life a ransom for many."* and *Matt 20:28, "Even as the Son of man came not to be ministered unto, but to minister, and to give his life a ransom for many."* and *Jn 13:15, "For I have given you an example, that ye should do as I have done to you."* and *1 Pet 2:21, "For even here unto were ye called: because Christ also suffered for us, leaving us an example, that ye should follow his steps:"*

All of Jesus' teachings were more than words, He walked His talk, so we can believe and follow His example, *Eph 5:25, "Husbands, love your wives, even as Christ also loved the church, and gave himself for it;"* Patience, sacrifice and love lead us to the selfless life Jesus led. He came to show us the way, *Matt 7:13-14, "Enter ye in at the strait gate: for wide is the gate, and broad is the way, that leadeth to destruction, and many there be which go in thereat. Because strait is the gate, and narrow is the way, which leadeth unto life, and few there be that find it."* The way is marked for the servant, *Matt 25:23, "His lord said unto him, Well done, good and faithful servant; thou hast been faithful over a few things, I will make thee ruler over many things: enter thou into the joy of thy lord."*

He told us to love in a way many did not understand, then He showed us the ultimate example of forgiveness on the cross, *Lk 23:34, "Then said Jesus, Father, forgive them; for they know not what they do. And they parted his raiment, and cast lots."*

6 - To teach us not to fear, *Matt 10:28, "And fear not them which kill the body, but are not able to kill the soul: but rather fear him which is able to destroy both soul and body in hell."* Only God has power over the second death and the eternity of our souls, *Heb 4:12, "For the word of God is quick, and powerful, and sharper than any twoedged sword, piercing even to the dividing asunder of soul and spirit, and of the joints and marrow, and is a discerner of the thoughts and intents of the heart."* Jesus came to teach us to love everyone and to fear no one, *1 Jn 4:18, "There is no fear in love; but perfect love casteth out fear: because fear hath torment. He that feareth is not made perfect in love."* and *Ps 27:1, "The Lord is my light and my salvation; whom shall I fear? the Lord is the strength of my life; of whom shall I be afraid?"*

When we understand Jesus is the Son of God and accept Him as our savior, we will fear no one, *Is 41:10, "Fear thou not; for I am with thee: be not dismayed; for I am thy God: I will strengthen thee; yea, I will help thee; yea, I will uphold thee with the right hand of my righteousness."* Job has the answer, *Job 33:12, "Behold, in this thou art not just: I will answer thee, that God is greater than man."* King David understood, *Ps 27:1, "The Lord is my light and my salvation; whom shall I fear? the Lord is the strength of my life; of whom shall I be afraid?"*

Fear leads us to bondage, this is the very reason those bringing evil use terrorism as their weapon. Jesus came to experience all temptation and pain, so that we could understand He has the power to free us from the second death, *Heb 2:14-15, "Forasmuch then as the children are partakers of flesh and blood, he also himself likewise took part of the same; that through death he might destroy him that had the power of death, that is, the devil; And deliver them who through fear of death were all their lifetime subject to bondage."*

The devil will bring us tribulations to create doubt and fear, in hopes he might separate us from our love of God, *Rev 2:10-11, "Fear none of those things which thou shalt suffer: behold, the devil shall cast some of you into prison, that ye may be tried; and ye shall have tribulation ten days: be thou faithful unto death, and I will give thee a crown of life. He that hath an ear, let him hear what the Spirit saith unto the churches; He that overcometh shall not be hurt of the second death."* God is with us through all of the tribulations we face, if we will only open our hearts enough to see Him in the fire with us, *Dan 3:25, "He answered and said, Lo, I see four men loose, walking in the midst of the fire, and they have no hurt; and the form of the fourth is like the Son of God."* We need not fear, God is with us and will keep us from the second death!

7 - To teach us how to live abundantly, *Ps 36:7-9, "How excellent is thy lovingkindness, O God! therefore the children of men put their trust under the shadow of thy wings. They shall be abundantly satisfied with the fatness of thy house; and thou shalt make them drink of the river of thy pleasures. For with thee is the fountain of life: in thy light shall we see light."* and *Jn 10:10, "The thief cometh not, but for to steal, and to kill, and to destroy: I am come that they might have life, and that they might*

have it more abundantly." Jesus wants us to live an abundant life, not just in this world, but also in the world to come.

So, what is an abundant life? God tells us it is the fullness of joy, Ps 16:11, *"Thou wilt shew me the path of life: in thy presence is fulness of joy; at thy right hand there are pleasures for evermore."* The fullness of joy comes from being in God's presence. I once explained to my wife, Gail, that when she is in the room I am happy, I have a sense of peace. Even when we are not talking, even when we are each involved in our own activities. Moreover, I do not have the same sense of peace doing that same activity when I am alone. No matter what the activity, it is better when I am with her. This feeling of being whole, being one, is the one God intended for us when He created us to become one flesh. It is the same feeling we get when we are truly in the presence of God. It is the fullness of joy!

Solomon explains the problem of trying to get this feeling any other way, in Ecclesiastes, which he wrote in 931 BC. Solomon, who had wealth beyond imagination, tried using his wealth to bring him joy, he experimented with every pleasure, he studied all knowledge available to him, in the end he came to the conclusion it was all vanity. Humans trying to do anything independent of God find themselves enveloped in foolishness. Leaving God out of our thinking leaves us only the devices of men and we can never find true satisfaction on that path; no matter how much wealth we have, no matter how much pleasure we enjoy, and no matter how much knowledge we acquire. We must follow the path that God has created for us, if we want to live an abundant life of peace and joy,

Eccl 12:8-14, "Vanity of vanities, saith the preacher; all is vanity. And moreover, because the preacher was wise, he still taught the people knowledge; yea, he gave good heed, and sought out, and set in order many proverbs. The preacher sought to find out acceptable words: and that which was written was upright, even words of truth. The words of the wise are as goads, and as nails fastened by the masters of assemblies, which are given from one shepherd. And further, by these, my son, be admonished: of making many books there is no end; and much study is a weariness of the flesh. Let us hear the conclusion of the whole matter: Fear God, and keep his commandments: for this is the whole duty of man. For God shall bring every work into judgment, with every secret thing, whether it be good, or whether it be evil."

Jesus told us in, *Jn 10:14 "I am the good shepherd, and know my sheep, and am known of mine."* He is the good shepherd that shows us the way! Jesus, also told us in, *Lk 11:31 "The queen of the south shall rise up in the judgment with the men of this generation, and condemn them: for she came from the utmost parts of the earth to hear the wisdom of Solomon; and, behold, a greater than Solomon is here."* Jesus is the Truth Solomon found, the good shepherd.

God knows worrying prevents us from enjoying an abundant life, so, we are to forget the worries of the past; the things we have said, the things we have done, the people we have hurt; and focus on the good that He has promised, *Lk 9:62, "And Jesus said unto him, No man, having put his hand to the plough, and looking back, is fit for the kingdom of God."* When we have confessed our sins, repented from them, and forgiven those who have harmed us, we are to forget the troubles of the past, and then we will be free to maximize the enjoyment of our present life and our future life!

The abundant life comes from our residing in the presence of God!

8 – Jesus came to bring the fire of baptism, *Matt 3:11, "I indeed baptize you with water unto repentance. but he that cometh after me is mightier than I, whose shoes I am not worthy to bear: he shall baptize you with the Holy Ghost, and with fire:"* John the Baptist tells us that Jesus is the one that baptizes with fire. When we do accept Jesus as our savior, we will know the truth of that statement, because we will begin to hear the Comforter God has sent to help us when we reason with His Living Word, *Jn 14:26, "But the Comforter, which is the Holy Ghost, whom the Father will send in my name, he shall teach you all things, and bring all things to your remembrance, whatsoever I have said unto you."*

Jesus goes on to explain that the fire He brings will divide us into two groups, those who choose to believe and those who refuse to even reason with Him, *Lk 12:49-56, "I am come to send fire on the earth; and what will I, if it be already kindled? But I have a baptism to be baptized with; and how am I straitened till it be accomplished! Suppose ye that I am come to give peace on earth? I tell you, Nay; but rather division: For from henceforth there shall be five in one house divided, three against two, and two against three. The father shall be divided against the son, and the son against the father; the mother against the daughter, and the daughter against the mother; the mother in law against her daughter in law, and the daughter in law against her mother in law. And he said also* to the people, *When ye see a cloud rise out of the west, straightway ye say, There cometh a shower; and so it is. And when ye see the south wind blow, ye say, There will be heat; and it cometh to pass. Ye hypocrites, ye can discern the face of the sky and of the earth; but how is it that ye do not discern this time?"* The divisions described here are part of the evidence He has left us, to help us find Him in our world. All we need to do is look around, are families divided on this issue? What has caused millions of people to believe in Jesus? This is one of the reasons the devil is working to divide us on so many other issues, like race or religion or sex or age, etc., he is trying to mask the only division that really matters.

9 - To fulfill prophecy by fulfilling the law and the prophets, *Matt 5:17-18, "Think not that I am come to destroy the law, or the prophets: I am not come to destroy, but to fulfil. For verily I say unto you, Till heaven and earth pass, one jot or one tittle shall in no wise pass from the law, till all be fulfilled."* and *Rom 15:8, "Now I say that Jesus Christ was a minister of the circumcision for the truth of God, to confirm the promises made unto the fathers:"* Jesus came to fulfill all of the prophecies and to live the life that the prophets had prophesied, *Jn 5:46, "For had ye believed Moses, ye would have believed me; for he wrote of me."* God has always known that those of us who think ourselves wise would not believe Moses and would not believe Jesus.

Lk 24:44, "And he said unto them, These are the words which I spake unto you, while I was yet with you, that all things must be fulfilled, which were written in the law of Moses, and in the prophets, and in the psalms, concerning me." This is yet another part of the proof He left for us to find Him.

10 - To die on the cross for our sins as a ransom for us, *Matt 20:28, "Even as the Son of man came not to be ministered unto, but to minister, and to give his life a ransom for many."* and *Jn 1:29, "The next day John seeth Jesus coming unto him, and saith, Behold the Lamb of God, which taketh away the sin of the world."* and *1 Jn 3:5, "And ye know that he was manifested to take away our sins; and in him is no sin."* and *Heb 9:26, "For then must he often have suffered since the foundation of the world: but now once in the end of the world hath he appeared to put away sin by the sacrifice of himself."* and *Rom 6:23, "For the wages of sin is death; but the gift of God is eternal life through Jesus Christ our Lord."*

Jesus has offered all of us the choice, the only thing keeping us from eternity is our finally making the decision, *1 Jn 2:2, "And he is the propitiation for our sins: and not for ours only, but also for the sins of the whole world."* He did not die for some of us or just the elect; He died for the whole world.

He died so we could live, both in this life and the next, *Heb 2:9, "But we see Jesus, who was made a little lower than the angels for the suffering of death, crowned with glory and honour; that he by the grace of God should taste death for every man."* and *Col 1:20, "And, having made peace through the blood of his cross, by him to reconcile all things unto himself; by him, I say, whether they be things in earth, or things in heaven."* His death removed the veil that separated us from God, *Eph 1:13-14, "But now in Christ Jesus ye who sometimes were far off are made nigh by the blood of Christ. For he is our peace, who hath made both one, and hath broken down the middle wall of partition between us;"* Thus, reconciling all things with His precious blood on the cross, *1 Pet 1:18-19, "Forasmuch as ye know that ye were not redeemed with corruptible things, as silver and gold, from your vain conversation received by tradition from your fathers; But with the precious blood of Christ, as of a lamb without blemish and without spot:"*

Jesus willingly went to the cross for all who will choose to sow to the Spirit and not to the flesh, *Gal 6:8-9, "For he that soweth to his flesh shall of the flesh reap corruption; but he that soweth to the Spirit shall of the Spirit reap life everlasting. And let us not be weary in well doing: for in due season we shall reap, if we faint not."* Honestly reasoning with His Word leads us to the Spirit of Truth, *Jn 16:13, "Howbeit when he, the Spirit of truth, is come, he will guide you into all truth: for he shall not speak of himself; but whatsoever he shall hear, that shall he speak: and he will shew you things to come."*

He told us people would hate us because of our belief, *Matt 10:22, "And ye shall be hated of all men for my name's sake: but he that endureth to the end shall be saved."* We cannot let them turn us from His love, but rather we must be steadfast until the end, *Heb 3:14, "For we are made partakers of Christ, if we hold the beginning of our confidence stedfast unto the end;"* so, we can partake of His reward, *1 Jn 2:24-25, "Let that therefore abide in you, which ye have heard from the beginning. If that which ye have heard from the beginning shall remain in you, ye also shall continue in the Son, and in the Father. And this is the promise that he hath promised us, even eternal life."*

He endured the cross to save us from our sins, *Heb 12:1-5,* *"Wherefore seeing we also are compassed about with so great a cloud of witnesses, let us lay aside every weight, and the sin which doth so easily beset us, and let us run with patience the race that is set before us, Looking unto Jesus the author and finisher of our faith; who for the joy that was set before him endured the cross, despising the shame, and is set down at the right hand of the throne of God. For consider him that endured such contradiction of sinners against himself, lest ye be wearied and faint in your minds. Ye have not yet resisted unto blood, striving against sin. And ye have forgotten the exhortation which speaketh unto you as unto children, My son, despise not thou the chastening of the Lord, nor faint when thou art rebuked of him:"* People are watching us to see if we truly believe He has saved us from our sins. Are we enduring our crosses?

11 - To destroy the works of the devil, *1 Jn 3:8,* *"He that committeth sin is of the devil; for the devil sinneth from the beginning. For this purpose the Son of God was manifested, that he might destroy the works of the devil."*

By destroying the works of the devil, Jesus is bringing us the kingdom of God, *Matt 12:28,* *"But if I cast out devils by the Spirit of God, then the kingdom of God is come unto you."* When we are released from the devil's bondage, we are able to seek God's righteousness and to enjoy His bounty, *Matt 6:33,* *"But seek ye first the kingdom of God, and his righteousness; and all these things shall be added unto you."*

We must be vigilant, the devil is frantically working to lead us away from God, *1 Pet 5:8, "Be sober, be vigilant; because your adversary the devil, as a roaring lion, walketh about, seeking whom he may devour:"*

12 - From the comfort of heaven, *2 Cor 8:9, "For ye know the grace of our Lord Jesus Christ, that, though he was rich, yet for your sakes he became poor, that ye through his poverty might be rich."* and *Phil 2:6-8, "Who, being in the form of God, thought it not robbery to be equal with God: But made himself of no reputation, and took upon him the form of a servant, and was made in the likeness of men: And being found in fashion as a man, he humbled himself, and became obedient unto death, even the death of the cross.",* He left the riches of His throne and knew He would have to face death on the cross, but He came anyway.

Jesus knew what He was facing and He came anyway. The drops of blood that fell from His brow in the garden testified to the anguish He felt, *Lk 22:44, "And being in an agony he prayed more earnestly: and his sweat was as it were great drops of blood falling down to the ground."* What more need He do?

The Last Days?

To understand the last days, we must first understand the four major events that divide time. The first event was the creation of this world and it marked the beginning of time. About, two thousand years later God brought us a worldwide flood to restart the creation process, Then, some two thousand years later Jesus came to offer salvation to all. And, finally, after another period of about two thousand years, He will return to collect all who have accepted His invitation. This period of time between His two visits is the period the Bible calls "the last days," *Heb 1:1-2, "God, who at sundry times and in divers manners spake in time past unto the fathers by the prophets, Hath in these last days spoken unto us by his Son, whom he hath appointed heir of all things, by whom also he made the worlds;"* Jesus was manifested for these last days, *1 Pet 1:20, "Who verily was foreordained before the foundation of the world, but was manifest in these last times for you,"* This final period, where God finishes the creation of His eternal family, is marked by the bookend appearances of His son Jesus.

Jesus is the central theme separating the last days from the rest of time and He came for us. Only after His first coming could people have the opportunity to accept Him as their savior. During Old Testament times, people had to accept the Messiah who was to come, even though they did not understand that His first coming would be in the form of a Lamb, not the Lion of Judah they were expecting, *Job 19:25-26*, *"For I know that my redeemer liveth, and that he shall stand at the latter day upon the earth: And though after my skin worms destroy this body, yet in my flesh shall I see God:"* Job knew he would see his savior, his redeemer, on the last day. He did not know that Jesus would first come to be sacrificed, and then some two thousand years later return for that last day. This is why many did not recognize Him, *Matt 16:2-3*, *"He answered and said unto them, When it is evening, ye say, It will be fair weather: for the sky is red. And in the morning, It will be foul weather to day: for the sky is red and lowering. O ye hypocrites, ye can discern the face of the sky; but can ye not discern the signs of the times?"* They should have known, for He told them, He came to fulfill all the prophecies and He had to come first as a Lamb to die for our sins. When He returns, He will be the Lion of Judah and our King. This is the mystery that was hidden from those in Old Testament times, *Col 1:23-28*, *"If ye continue in the faith grounded and settled, and be not moved away from the hope of the gospel, which ye have heard, and which was preached to every creature which is under heaven; whereof I Paul am made a minister; Who now rejoice in my sufferings for you, and fill up that which is behind of the afflictions of Christ in my flesh for his body's sake, which is the church: Whereof I am made a minister, according to the dispensation of God which is given to me for you, to fulfil the word of God; Even the mystery which hath been hid from ages and from generations, but now is made manifest to his saints: To whom God would make known what is the riches of the glory of this mystery among the Gentiles; which is Christ in you, the hope of glory: Whom we preach, warning every man, and teaching every man in all wisdom; that we may present every man perfect in Christ Jesus:"*

Eccl 3:11, "He hath made every thing beautiful in his time: also he hath set the world in their heart, so that no man can find out the work that God maketh from the beginning to the end." No man can know everything God has done to make sure His plan is completed. But, that does not mean we cannot know what He has left for us to know. We do this by studying His Word, *2 Tim 2:15, "Study to shew thyself approved unto God, a workman that needeth not to be ashamed, rightly dividing the word of truth."* When two honestly come together to reason with God regarding different understandings of His Word, the Truth will become evident, *Matt 18:20, "For where two or three are gathered together in my name, there am I in the midst of them."* First, we must come together in love, invite the Holy Spirit to help us discern the Truth of the matter and finally we need to pray that we will accept the Truth the Holy Spirit brings us, *Jn 16:13, "Howbeit when he, the Spirit of truth, is come, he will guide you into all truth: for he shall not speak of himself; but whatsoever he shall hear, that shall he speak: and he will shew you things to come."*

There are many elements to these last days and we will devote this chapter to the idea of reasoning with God to better understand those elements. We start with the beginning of these last days, the period from when Jesus began His ministry to the time the disciples began fulfilling their charge of spreading the gospel.

The manifestation of Jesus signaled the call to unity, not just for the Jews but all humanity. Each of us has been offered salvation and when we accept this offer, we need to work together to do our part in His plan for salvation. This is the process of becoming one body,

1 Cor 12:13, *"For by one Spirit are we all baptized into one body, whether we be Jews or Gentiles, whether we be bond or free; and have been all made to drink into one Spirit."* When we accept His offer of salvation we will begin to feel the call to complete our part in His plan. Doing our part means we begin to experience the promise of a good life, now and for all eternity, *1 Tim 4:8, "For bodily exercise profiteth little: but godliness is profitable unto all things, having promise of the life that now is, and of that which is to come."*

When Jesus' disciples came to Him asking how they would know the time of the end of the world, He told them about the beginning of sorrows, a list of the types of events the world could watch to monitor the progress toward the end of time, *Matt 24:8, "All these are the beginning of sorrows."* The "beginning of sorrows" parallels the birthing process, as described in *chapter 13 of Isaiah*.[67] As the last days progress, both the frequency and severity of the events will increase. But, even in the beginning of the birth process there still is pain, as the disciples would personally experience. So we can mark this early period as the beginning of sorrows.

Lk 17:21, "Neither shall they say, Lo here! or, lo there! for, behold, the kingdom of God is within you." Jesus' arrival at the beginning of the last days means that each of us can begin living the kingdom of God today, by simply accepting Him as our savior. This does not mean we will not suffer during these last days, as we do our part in His plan. The enemy, the devil, will do whatever he can to make it difficult for us to complete our part in God's plan, *Matt 10:22, "And ye shall be hated of all men for my name's sake: but he that endureth to the end shall be saved."* If we keep our eyes on the mission God has ordained for us, He will return and save us. *Jn 14:1-3, "Let not your heart be troubled: ye believe in God, believe also in me. In my Father's house are many mansions: if it were not so, I would have told you. I go to prepare a place for you. And if I go and prepare a place for you, I will come again, and receive you unto myself; that where I am, there ye may be also."* He promised He is coming again!

The period following Jesus' crucifixion to the end of the first century was the first phase of the formation of Christ's church, *Rev 22:16, "I Jesus have sent mine angel to testify unto you these things in the churches. I am the root and the offspring of David, and the bright and morning star."* Jesus sent His angel to prophesy to John regarding the seven churches and this prophecy includes His return at the end of the last church period.

The first church period John tells us about was the **"Church of Ephesus"**, *Rev 2:1-7, "Unto the angel of the church of Ephesus write; These things saith he that holdeth the seven stars in his right hand, who walketh in the midst of the seven golden candlesticks; I know thy works, and thy labour, and thy patience, and how thou canst not bear them which are evil: and thou hast tried them which say they are apostles, and are not, and hast found them liars: And hast borne, and hast patience, and for my name's sake hast laboured, and hast not fainted. Nevertheless I have somewhat against thee, because thou hast left thy first love. Remember therefore from whence thou art fallen, and repent, and do the first works; or else I will come unto thee quickly, and will remove thy candlestick out of his place, except thou repent. But this thou hast, that thou hatest the deeds* *of the Nicolaitanes, which I also hate. He that hath an ear, let him hear what the Spirit saith unto the churches; To him that overcometh will I give to eat of the tree of life, which is in the midst of the paradise of God."*

Jesus is telling us, in John's writings, that this first century church, the forerunner to the Roman Catholic Church, began by doing good works. They reasoned with the Word of God to test what was being preached by different people and denounced those who were not sticking to the Truth. However, before the century ended, the collective teachings had drifted from the teachings of Jesus. He was calling them back to their first love, Him and His Word. He asked them to repent and to return to their first works, the works He called them to prior to His resurrection. He told them this was the only way to eternal life, as He at the same time is telling us. This is an example of the principle of layers, like the layers of an onion, as Jesus teaches lessons in each verse, the meaning is multiplied by other verses in the Bible. Jesus is not just talking to that first century church; He is teaching people throughout time, including us today. This principle, of reasoning with the Truth, is one of the most important messages in the Bible and is repeated many times. *Is 28:9-10, "Whom shall he teach knowledge? and whom shall he make to understand doctrine? them that are weaned from the milk, and drawn from the breasts. For precept must be upon precept, precept upon precept; line upon line, line upon line; here a little, and there a little:"*

John continues on to the second church period, which Jesus calls the **"Church of Smyrna"**, *Rev 2:8-11, "And unto the angel of the church in Smyrna write; These things saith the first and the last, which was dead,* *and is alive; I know thy works, and tribulation, and poverty, (but thou art rich) and I know the blasphemy of them which say they are Jews, and are not, but are the synagogue of Satan. Fear none of those things which thou shalt suffer: behold, the devil shall cast some of you into prison, that ye may be tried; and ye shall have tribulation ten days: be thou faithful unto death, and I will give thee a crown of life. He that hath an ear, let him hear what the Spirit saith unto the churches; He that overcometh shall not be hurt of the second death."*

The Church of Smyrna covered the period from 100 AD to 311 AD, which ended with a ten-year period of terrifying persecution by Diocletian and Galerius. These two Roman Emperors so persecuted the church that this last ten-year period came to be known as the "Age of Martyrdom." There are no condemnations for this church in John's message to us. Even though the church faced poverty and persecution, it had returned to Jesus and the mission He gave them, unto death. John's message regarding this church was written as prophecy, just as this church period was beginning. This prophecy was written for everyone, so that we might witness the martyrdom and draw strength from it. Notice that John tells us that even though this church was poor, void of expensive churches or lavish lifestyles, and persecuted unto martyrdom, they were rich because they stayed faithful to God's Word. He also points out that there were others claiming to be Jews who were not following God's Word, but rather Satan and their own selfish desires. Each of us will face some level of persecution for our devotion to God's Word. The devil will not rest, but rather he will focus his evil on those who are leading others to the Truth, as Paul told us in, *Acts 14:22, "Confirming the souls of the disciples, and exhorting them to continue in the faith, and that we must through much tribulation enter into the kingdom of God."* Paul wants us to know we are to continue to confirm the souls of the disciples and exhort all who will listen to continue in the faith. He also wants us to recognize the church of Satan, those who claim to be Christians, but live their lives in defiance of God's Truth. This admonition is to avoid these churches, not to harm them. We can know them by their fruit, *Matt 7:16, "Ye shall know them by their fruits. Do men gather grapes of thorns, or figs of thistles?"* We can look around us and see those who spout hatred and do violent acts, avoid them and the church they worship, whether that church calls itself Christian or is the church of earthly rewards. The church of earthly rewards calls is to worship at the alters of power, fame, pleasure and wealth.

Some have asked why God allows His church to be persecuted. The answer is rather simple, He wants all of us to have the chance to choose to be part of His eternal family and we can only do that if we can see the difference between the good He has promised and the evil that is of the devil. When we honestly reason with the fruits of these two very different beings, we will choose God and His eternal family, *Matt 5:10-12, "Blessed are they which are persecuted for righteousness' sake: for theirs is the kingdom of heaven. Blessed are ye, when men shall revile you, and persecute you, and shall say all manner of evil against you falsely, for my sake. Rejoice, and be exceeding glad: for great is your reward in heaven: for so persecuted they the prophets which were before you."* Yes, only when we honestly reason with the fruits of both sides can we can recognize righteousness, and whatever the persecution that results in this life, it is a small price to pay to allow everyone the opportunity to see just how evil evil is. Remember, our time on this earth is but a small fraction of the eternity we will spend with God in heaven.

During the final years of this period, called the "Age of Martyrdom," those Roman emperors, Diocletian and Galerius, attempted to wipe out Christianity. Many have tried to kill Christianity over the years, but none have succeeded! Many in our own country are trying to do the same thing today. Why have so many ignored the fact that Christianity has survived to fulfill God's will? Why have the fulfillment of so many prophecies not opened the eyes, minds and hearts, of those who still deny Jesus?

Deut 4:30, "When thou art in tribulation, and all these things are come upon thee, even in the latter days, if thou turn to the Lord thy God, and shalt be obedient unto his voice; (For the Lord thy God is a merciful God;) he will not forsake thee, neither destroy thee, nor forget the covenant of thy fathers which he sware unto them." God was talking to Moses, however, if we are listening and can see the layers, He is also talking to us. His love and mercy are eternal, He will not forsake us, but it is always our choice. We can choose God and His love and mercy, or we can choose to ignore Him. The problem with ignoring Him is that anything but a vote for God is a vote for Satan. We cannot back into heaven; we must choose to be there! God has promised, *Jn 12:48, "He that rejecteth me, and receiveth not my words, hath one that judgeth him: the word that I have spoken, the same shall judge him in the last day."* and *Jn 6:40, "And this is the will of him that sent me, that every one which seeth the Son, and believeth on him, may have everlasting life: and I will raise him up at the last day."*

The **"Church in Pergamos"** is the next church and it covers the period from 311 AD to 538 AD, John wrote about this church some two centuries before the period began. John gives us Jesus' message to this church in, *Rev 2:12-17, "And to the angel of the church in Pergamos write; These things saith he which hath the sharp sword with two edges; I know thy works, and where thou dwellest, even where Satan's seat is: and thou holdest fast my name, and hast not denied my faith, even in those days wherein Antipas was my faithful martyr, who was slain among you, where Satan dwelleth. But I have a few things against thee, because thou hast there them that hold the doctrine of Balaam, who taught Balac to cast a stumblingblock before the children of Israel, to eat things sacrificed unto idols, and to commit fornication. So hast thou also them that hold the doctrine of the Nicolaitanes, which thing I hate. Repent; or else I will come unto thee quickly, and will fight against them with the sword of my mouth. He that hath an ear, let him hear what the Spirit saith unto the churches; To him that overcometh will I give to eat of the hidden manna, and will give him a white stone, and in the stone a new name written, which no man knoweth saving he that receiveth it."*

God is telling this church that He knows what they are doing. He commends them for holding His name dear and keeping the faith. Antipas was a martyr of Pergamos and represents all martyrs who withstand the false religions, holding fast to the Truth. God is warning all who will listen that He will fight against them with the two edged sword of His mouth, His Holy Word, if they become hypocrites by following the doctrine of the Nicolaitanes, like the Saccades and Pharisees, whom He criticized for their lack of humility, their lording over of His Truth and their polluting of His Word, 1 Pet 5:1-3, *"The elders which are among you I exhort, who am also an elder, and a witness of the sufferings of Christ, and also a partaker of the glory that shall be revealed: Feed the flock of God which is among you, taking the oversight thereof, not by constraint, but willingly; not for filthy lucre, but of a ready mind; Neither as being lords over God's heritage, but being examples to the flock."*

God wants all of us to stick to His Word, to do it humbly, to willingly show His love to the world with a ready mind, and not to create manmade ideas for the flock to follow. God cringes at the thought that some will act as lords over His Word, as have too many church leaders. God knew this would be the church that would try to change the times and days, *Rev 22:18-19, "For I testify unto every man that heareth the words of the prophecy of this book, If any man shall add unto these things, God shall add unto him the plagues that are written in this book: And if any man shall take away from the words of the book of this prophecy, God shall take away his part out of the book of life, and out of the holy city, and from the things which are written in this book."*

God is telling us to overcome those who are trying to pervert His Word, for He will reward those who withstand the perversion with His hidden manna. He is calling all of us to follow the Holy

Ghost and to feed His flock with the Living Word, for He purchased this flock with His own blood, *Acts 20:28-30, "Take heed therefore unto yourselves, and to all the flock, over the which the Holy Ghost hath made you overseers, to feed the church of God, which he hath purchased with his own blood. For I know this, that after my departing shall grievous wolves enter in among you, not sparing the flock. Also of your own selves shall men arise, speaking perverse things, to draw away disciples after them."*

When we follow the Holy Ghost, we become servants to the Truth, honest followers who would not pollute the Truth, *Rom 6:22, "But now being made free from sin, and become servants to God, ye have your fruit unto holiness, and the end everlasting life."* We can try to fool ourselves, but in this life we will either become servants of God and His Truth, or we will at some level become slaves to the evil of the devil and willing participants in the pollution of God's Word, *Rom 6:16, "Know ye not, that to whom ye yield yourselves servants to obey, his servants ye are to whom ye obey; whether of sin unto death, or of obedience unto righteousness?"* God knew this church period would dwell where Satan's seat is, a place within the church that pollutes God's Word, blending the devil's lies with God's Truth, as did one of histories most influential Roman Emperors.

Roman Emperor Constantine played a big role in this church period. He had been introduced to Christianity when he was sent with his mother to the Eastern provinces. He embraced this new religion Christianity early in his military/political career. He bore a standard of a cross into his battles and won all of them on his rise to Emperor. He credited his success to the Christian God. In the year

312 AD Constantine became Western Emperor, through a complex series of civil wars ending when he defeated his brother-in-law Maxentius and formed an alliance with Licinius, who was to become the Eastern Emperor. They erected a statue in Rome with him holding up a cross to commemorate his victory. So, now there was a new Roman leader who believed in the power of Christianity. At that time the Roman Empire had factions of various pagan sun-worshipers and several Christian sects. Constantine dreamed of uniting all these varying parts of his empire. Not wanting to offend the Christian God, he needed to figure out a way to meld the competing ideas into one Roman religion.

In 321 AD he enacted a law establishing Sunday as the day of rest, making it unlawful for Christians to rest on Saturday, the Sabbath they were honoring. This was an appeasement to the sun-worshipers, who rested on Sunday. To finalize his plans to merge the two into one national religion he defeated his alley Licinius in 324 AD and called for the first Ecumenical Council, the Council of Nicaea, to form the first uniform Christian doctrine. In 325 AD Pope Sylvester named Sunday as the Lord's Day, however, it was not until the Council of Laodicea, 363 AD to 364 AD, that the Bishops outlawed the keeping of the Saturday Sabbath. This was some 25 years after Constantine's death, but it was the culmination of the work he started in 321 AD. The Council of Laodicea also specified the Biblical Canon, adding seven books that were not in the Jewish Torah, to create a new Old Testament. There was also the matter of keeping the Sabbath as commanded in the Ten Commandments. So, a couple of changes were made to the Ten Commandments. The fourth commandment was changed from "Remember the Sabbath Day by keeping it holy." to the third commandment "Remember to keep holy the Lord's Day." They also removed the second commandment and divided the tenth commandment into two to create the appearance of the original Ten Commandments. The devil had infiltrated the church and fulfilled the prophecy of the "Church of Peragamos."

Thus begins the age of compromise, where the Truth of God's Word would be continually watered down with lies. We today might recognize this idea of compromise, as we are told that compromising our beliefs is acceptable in the name of uniting people, even if it leads us all away from God. God is clearly declaring He hates this thing! He calls to us, 2 Cor 6:15-17, "And what concord hath Christ with Belial? or what part hath he that believeth with an infidel? And what agreement hath the temple of God with idols? for ye are the temple of the living God; as God hath said, I will dwell in them, and walk in them; and I will be their God, and they shall be my people. Wherefore come out from among them, and be ye separate, saith the Lord, and touch not the unclean thing; and I will receive you." The idols referred to in these verses are the ones the church began using when it removed the original second commandment, Ex 20:4-6, "Thou shalt not make unto thee any graven image, or any likeness of any thing that is in heaven above, or that is in the earth beneath, or that is in the water under the earth. Thou shalt not bow down thyself to them, nor serve them: for I the Lord thy God am a jealous God, visiting the iniquity of the fathers *upon the children unto the third and fourth generation of them that hate me; And shewing mercy unto thousands of them that love me, and keep my commandments."*

Next came the **"Church in Thyatira"** covering the period from 538 AD to the end of the dark ages in the sixteenth-century. This was the period that the Roman Catholic Church reigned and its Popes were more powerful than the kings of the countries within its empire. The church suppressed any ideas that did not fit with its ever-changing form of Christianity. For those not familiar with the concept of an ever-changing form of Christianity, you might want to Google purgatory, indulgences, etc. God gave us these verses to describe this period, *Rev 2:18-29, "And unto the angel of the church in Thyatira write; These things saith the Son of God, who hath his eyes like unto a flame of fire, and his feet are like fine brass; I know thy works, and charity, and service, and faith, and thy patience, and thy works; and the last to be more than the first. Notwithstanding I have a few things against thee, because thou sufferest that woman Jezebel, which calleth herself a prophetess, to teach and to seduce my servants to commit fornication, and to eat things sacrificed unto idols. And I gave her space to repent of her fornication; and she repented not. Behold, I will cast her into a bed, and them that commit adultery with her into great tribulation, except they repent of their deeds. And I will kill her children with death; and all the churches shall know that I am he which searcheth the reins and hearts: and I will give unto every one of you according to your works. But unto you I say, and unto the rest in Thyatira, as many as have not this doctrine, and which have not known the depths of Satan, as they speak; I will put upon you none other burden. But that which ye have already hold fast till I come.*

And he that overcometh, and keepeth my works unto the end, to him will I give power over the nations: And he shall rule them with a rod of iron; as the vessels of a potter shall they be broken to shivers: even as I received of my Father. And I will give him the morning star. He that hath an ear, let him hear what the Spirit saith unto the churches." This church period is marked by the few, the religious leaders of the time, attempting to produce the good ends God wants, by whatever means. Many innocent souls were tormented by their means.

God begins His analysis of this church by telling them that He sees everything, He knows their works, good and bad, and that those works will be exposed to the flame of His eyes. Nothing escapes His awareness, as nothing escapes the flames once placed into the fire. He tells them that the ends they are striving for are good: charity, service, faith and patience. He knows that they are working out of love for Christ. However, He also sees the means they are using to achieve those ends, like allowing Jezebel to enter into His church. Jezebel here is a reference to King Ahab's wife, who led Israel into Sun worshipping under the name of Baal, teaching and seducing the people. This deception was only possible because the Roman Catholic Church did not allow the people to read the Bible; they were to accept whatever the church told them, which was that part of God's Word that left room for the means being used. For this entire church period the church never repented from the sins God has against it. Many future Catholics would suffer from the deceit that was being used to justify the ends.

God promises He will not hold us accountable for the works of others, only our own works. He also tells us that He will search each person's heart and will reward us according to our own deeds. God sees through our false religious performances meant to fool others into thinking we are holy, *2 Cor 5:10, "For we must all appear before the judgment seat of Christ; that every one may receive the things done in his body, according to that he hath done, whether it be good or bad."*

God prophesied that the rest of His people, those not drawn to the works of Jezebel, would be rewarded for their faith! Those who did not follow Jezebel were represented by the Waldensians in mainland Europe, the followers of Wycliffe in England, and many others spread all over the Roman Catholic Empire. These faithful pioneers were busy translating the Word of God into their native languages and delivering the Truth, by hand and mouth to all the people who were willing to listen. This was in defiance of the Roman Catholic Church and many died for their work. Link to: Roman Catholic Persecution Of Reformers.[68]

The next church of the Last Days was the **"Church in Sardis"** covering the period from the sixteenth-century to 1798 AD and John gives us Jesus' message to this church in, *Rev 3:1-6, "And unto the angel of the church in Sardis write; These things saith he that hath the seven Spirits of God, and the seven stars; I know thy works, that thou hast a name that thou livest, and art dead. Be watchful, and strengthen the things which remain, that are ready to die: for I have not found thy works perfect before God. Remember therefore how thou hast received and heard, and hold fast, and repent. If therefore thou shalt not watch, I will come on* *thee as a thief, and thou shalt not know what hour I will come upon thee. Thou hast a few names even in Sardis which have not defiled their garments; and they shall walk with me in white: for they are worthy. He that overcometh, the same shall be clothed in white raiment; and I will not blot out his name out of the book of life, but I will confess his name before my Father, and before his angels. He that hath an ear, let him hear what the Spirit saith unto the churches."*

God is telling us that this period marks the end of power for the Roman Catholic Church. The Protestant Reformation was one of those things that remained, where strength in God's Word exposed the false teachings of the Roman Catholic Church and caused the church to lose its hold over the kings of the countries within its empire. The dangerous hard work performed by the Waldensians, Wycliffe and so many more would finally come to fruition with Luther, Calvin, Zwingli and many more, who opened the eyes of the people to the Truth hidden from them for so long. This new church took the name of Protestant, as they protested against the Roman Catholic Church and proclaimed salvation by faith through one name, Jesus Christ. This noble Protestant beginning crumbled under the divisions of doctrine and subsequent creation of denominations. God is telling us that this church is dead, because it could not find a united way to the Truth, to becoming one body. The leaders stopped reasoning with God, as He has so often asked, Is 1:18, *"Come now, and let us reason together, saith the Lord: though your sins be as scarlet, they shall be as white as snow; though they be red like crimson, they shall be as wool."* When we lay down our pride and come to God to honestly reason with His Truth, we will always be led to the universal Truth that is His. It is Satan that builds up our pride which leads us to the divisions that weaken our view of the Truth, for we are stronger when we come together united by the Truth. *Eccl 4:12, "And if one prevail against him, two shall withstand him; and a threefold cord is not quickly broken."* This new movement led many away from the Roman Catholic Church which sparked a Catholic counter-movement, led by the Jesuits, which began by trying to re-interpret scripture. The Jesuits hated the Protestant movement and set out to destroy it. The Jesuit's work can be seen in our modern society; the introduction of the rapture, the changing of the end times Israel prophecies, the coming of the antichrist, etc. For more on: Jesuits Re-interpret Scripture.[69]

Unfortunately, once the new Protestant movement established itself as a worldwide force, it became satisfied with the accomplishment. There was no longer a desire to continue growing spiritually, no longer a fire to unite the church into one body. Faith in Christ was enough. This salvation through faith alone has led the Protestant movement away from the concepts of works. But, Jesus' teaching on this point was clear, *Jam 2:17-20, "Even so faith, if it hath not works, is dead, being alone. Yea, a man may say, Thou hast faith, and I have works: shew me thy faith without thy works, and I will shew thee my faith by my works. Thou believest that there is one God; thou doest well: the devils also believe, and tremble. But wilt thou know, O vain man, that faith without works is dead?"* Jesus warned us that leaving love out of His Truth leaves us with an empty facade of religion, rather that the true love and faith that always leads to works, *Matt 7:22-23, "Many will say to me in that day, Lord, Lord, have we not prophesied in thy name? and in thy name have cast out devils? and in thy name done many wonderful works? And then will I profess unto them, I never knew you: depart from me, ye that work iniquity."* This is the main reason John says this church is dead. Works are the fruit of our faith, without works there is no real faith. True faith touches the heart in a way that we are inescapably drawn to works, for those works help others see God's love for them. God wants us to do these works for the right reason, because we love Him and want to shine His light. When we distort this concept and use it to show others how pious we are, we are doing the works for the wrong reasons, as we see in these two sets of verses, *Matt 6:1-4, "Take heed that ye do not your alms before men, to be seen of them: otherwise ye have no reward of your Father which is in heaven. Therefore when thou doest thine alms, do not sound a trumpet before thee, as the hypocrites do in the synagogues and in the streets, that they may have glory of men. Verily I say unto you, They have their reward. But when thou doest alms, let not thy left hand know what thy right hand doeth: That thine alms may be in secret: and thy Father which seeth in secret himself shall reward thee openly."* and *Matt 5:16, "Let your light so shine before men, that they may see your good works, and glorify your Father which is in heaven."*

God is asking all churches to examine their motives, to repent from their evil deeds and to return to the Truth of His Word, without changing or distorting it. God loved the Protestant movement even before its humble beginnings. A small seed made up of a few humble people, hiding, and copying the original scriptures into all languages and then taking the Word to every corner of civilization. We all need to thank Peter Waldo, John Wycliffe, Jan Hus, Martin Luther, John Calvin, Huldrych Zwingli, and so many more that did the works God called them to do without worldly reward and in the face of death. This church period ended when Napolean's general Berthier entered Rome with an army, captured Pope Pius VI and abolished the Papacy. This is the exact date prophesied by Daniel in, *Dan 7:25, "And he shall speak great words against the most High, and shall wear out the saints of the most High, and think to change times and laws: and they shall be given into his hand until a time and times and the dividing of time."* There is no doubt the Roman Catholic Church wore out the saints during this 1,260-year period from 538 AD to 1798 AD. Link to: Calculation Of The 1,260 Years of Daniel.[70]

Next came the **"Church in Philadelphia"** covering the period from 1798 AD to 1844 AD, *Rev 3:7-13, "And to the angel of the church in Philadelphia write; These things saith he that is holy, he that is true, he that hath the key of David, he that openeth, and no man shutteth; and shutteth, and no man openeth; I know thy works: behold, I have set before thee an open door, and no man can shut it: for thou hast a little strength, and hast kept my word, and hast not denied my name. Behold, I will make them of the synagogue of Satan, which say they are Jews, and are not, but do lie; behold, I will make them to come and worship before thy feet, and to know that I have loved thee. Because thou hast kept the word of my patience, I also will keep thee from the hour of temptation, which shall* *come upon all the world, to try them that dwell upon the earth. Behold, I come quickly: hold that fast which thou hast, that no man take thy crown. Him that overcometh will I make a pillar in the temple of my God, and he shall go no more out: and I will write upon him the name of my God, and the name of the city of my God, which is new Jerusalem, which cometh down out of heaven from my God: and I will write upon him my new name. He that hath an ear, let him hear what the Spirit saith unto the churches."*

God has no rebukes for this church. He is describing a church with little strength, a small church with few followers as the period begins. This church has kept the Word of God, loves His name, and is a true servant of God, continuing to seek a deeper understanding of His Truth. These are the true spiritual Jews whom He has called to be patient and obedient, to wait on His timing for all things. This church is ready and able to open the book of Daniel and to understand the prophecies in both Daniel and Revelation, which have been hidden for all these years. *Dan 12:4, "But thou, O Daniel, shut up the words, and seal the book, even to the time of the end: many shall run to and fro, and knowledge shall be increased."* This deeper understanding will bring to life the coming of the New Jerusalem and what life will be like for those who overcome, for those who wait on the Lord and patiently follow His calling. This church will long for heaven and the eternal life God promises above the temporary rewards of this world.

We now go to those newly opened books, Daniel and Revelation to help us understand the significance of the year 1844 AD? *Dan 7:1,*

10, *"In the first year of Belshazzar king of Babylon Daniel had a dream and visions of his head upon his bed: then he wrote the dream, and told the sum of the matters...A fiery stream issued and came forth from before him: thousand thousands ministered unto him, and ten thousand times ten thousand stood before him: the judgment was set, and the books were opened."* When will this judgment begin? *Dan 8:13-44, "Then I heard one saint speaking, and another saint said unto that certain saint which spake, How long shall be the vision concerning the daily sacrifice, and the transgression of desolation, to give both the sanctuary and the host to be trodden under foot? And he said unto me, Unto two thousand and three hundred days; then shall the sanctuary be cleansed."* What date do we add the 2,300 prophetic years to? *Dan 9:25, "Know therefore and understand, that from the going forth of the commandment to restore and to build Jerusalem unto the Messiah the Prince shall be seven weeks, and threescore and two weeks: the street shall be built again, and the wall, even in troublous times."* The going forth of the commandment from King Artaxerxes was the beginning point for both the 490-year prophecy and the 2,300-year prophecy and that date was 457 BC. as described in *Ezra 7*.[71] These facts give us the year 1844 AD as the date for the opening of the books and the beginning of the judgment. So this church period ends with millions of beings witnessing the opening of the door to the sanctuary, the most holy place. Then the books were opened, including the book of life, so that the judgment can begin in heaven. *Rev 11:19, "And the temple of God was opened in heaven, and there was seen in his temple the ark of his testament: and there were lightnings, and voices, and thunderings, and an earthquake, and great hail."* This is when Jesus applies His gift of salvation to all who have chosen to accept His blood as atonement for their sins, *Heb 9:12, "Neither by the blood of goats and calves, but by his own blood he entered in once into the holy place, having obtained eternal redemption for us."* Please notice it says He only entered once to obtain our eternal redemption. Here is a link to a more in-depth discussion on this subject: <u>Discussion Of The Year 1844 AD</u>.[72]

Phil 1:18, "What then? notwithstanding, every way, whether in pretence, or in truth, Christ is preached; and I therein do rejoice, yea, and will rejoice." Does this mean that God loves all churches? Yes, it means God loves any church that preaches Christ. Then why does He reprimand so many of them? To help inspire them to stick to the Truth, as any good father would. He wants all of us to stick to the Word He has given us. He wants the leaders of all churches to continue to reason with Him and correct the errors they are preaching and to work together to become one body in Christ. But, He loves the fact that many are opening the eyes and minds of non-believers, so they might learn about Jesus, who is our only way to salvation. Once we are introduced to Jesus, it is our individual responsibility to choose whether we will accept His offer of salvation, or reject it.

And so we come to the last church, the one we are living in today, the **"Church in Laodicea."** This church represents the period from 1844 AD, the beginning of judgment, the opening of the books, until the second coming of Jesus, *Rev 3:14-22, "And unto the angel of the church of the Laodiceans write; These things saith the Amen, the faithful and true witness, the beginning of the creation of God; I know thy* *works, that thou art neither cold nor hot: I would thou wert cold or hot. So then because thou art lukewarm, and neither cold nor hot, I will spue thee out of my mouth. Because thou sayest, I am rich, and increased with goods, and have need of nothing; and knowest not that thou art wretched, and miserable, and poor, and blind, and naked: I counsel thee to buy of me gold tried in the fire, that thou mayest be rich; and white raiment, that thou mayest be clothed, and that the shame of thy nakedness do not appear; and anoint thine eyes with eyesalve, that thou mayest see. As many as I love, I rebuke and chasten: be zealous therefore, and repent. Behold, I stand at the door, and knock: if any man hear my voice, and open the door, I will come in to him, and will sup with him, and he with me. To him that overcometh will I grant to sit with me in my throne, even as I also overcame, and am set down with my Father in his throne. He that hath an ear, let him hear what the Spirit saith unto the churches."*

Notice that this church receives no commendations, only rebukes. This church has settled into a comfortable place. There is no longer a fire for the Lord. The overall feeling is one of satisfaction with life as it is, nothing is needed, but God does not agree. He is telling this church that He loves it and rebukes it for it has fallen into a state of apathy; it has become lukewarm. He is calling this church to see how miserable, how poor, how blind, and how naked it has become. He wants this church to return to the study of His Word, to reason beyond the surface layers, to become hot for the Truth that lies beneath, to peel back the layers to the core and to return to the richness of the Truth first brought to light by the Luther's of this world. It is the opening of our eyes that allows us to see those deeper layers within the Bible. We cannot stay in our comfortable condition, naked in our sins, and without the works that are demanded by our faith, without the white-hot zeal for God's Truth, for God is telling us He will "spue" us out of His mouth. What would have happened if the people of Peter Waldo's day had not been white-hot for God's Word? God is troubled by how this church has wasted the light He has given it, light that was to be used to draw many to the Truth, like moths. The closer to the light we get, the warmer we feel, until the white-hot flame at the center burns our souls into action.

This lukewarm nature is selfish. It does not take into account the loss to others who will miss the message and the opportunity to find Jesus. *2 Tim 3:5, "Having a form of godliness, but denying the power thereof: from such turn away."* For who will be drawn to follow those they perceive as hypocrites. God tells us that everyone should turn away from those denying the power. Is there any wonder in the fact that so many have refused to listen to today's preachers? We cannot be satisfied with the fact that we have found Jesus; we must then be motivated to introduce Him to as many as we can. Too many today cite the hypocrites they see in our society, claiming to be Christians, as the reason they will not reason with God. They will not reason with God, because they cannot see God's light shining from those they perceive as hypocrites. We believers cannot hide in the comfort of our hypocrisy any longer. The time has come for us to take action, to let the world see God's love shining through us. To come together to correct the errors in our fundamental beliefs, to unite around God's fundamental beliefs, and to preach one Jesus, the Jesus who came to save us from our sins! Not everyone has fallen into this state of apathy, but far too many have.

He is standing at the door of every heart and He is knocking. It is up to each of us to make the decision, either open the door and enjoy eternity with Him, or ignore His knocking and live this life only, *Rev 3:20, "Behold, I stand at the door, and knock: if any man hear my voice, and open the door, I will come in to him, and will sup with him, and he with me."*

Rev 14:12, "Here is the patience of the saints: here are they that keep the commandments of God, and the faith of Jesus." Here is the key to living in these last days; we keep the commandments of God. We keep them because the world needs to see faithful people who love God and keep His commandments. The world does not need hypocrites who have faith without works. Our patience will draw others to Jesus when they are able to see that we truly love God enough to follow Him, to put up our treasures in heaven, rather than this world. They do not need to see us sporting our flashy bling, living in big homes, driving the best cars and dressed in the best clothes, they need to see us living the life God calls us to live, *Matt 6:19-21, "Lay not up for yourselves treasures upon earth, where moth and rust doth corrupt, and where thieves break through and steal: But lay up for yourselves treasures in heaven, where neither moth nor rust doth corrupt, and where thieves do not break through nor steal: For where your treasure is, there will your heart be also."* This is not to say we must be poor, for God has told us we cannot out give Him. He told us He loved David when David was the wealthiest person on the planet. God saw that David would come to understand that his relationship with God was more important than all the wealth he had accumulated. We are to give generously and focus on those who need our help, not on spending to have a comfortable life, alone. But, God has told us we can have both, if we first focus on doing His will, *Matt 6:31-34, "Therefore take no thought, saying, What shall we eat? or, What shall we drink? or, Wherewithal shall we be clothed? (For after all these things do the Gentiles seek:) for your heavenly Father knoweth that ye have need of all these things. But seek ye first the kingdom of God, and his righteousness; and all these things shall be added unto you. Take therefore no thought for the morrow: for the morrow shall take thought for the things of itself. Sufficient unto the day is the evil thereof."*

God's message is clear, when we care about others, He will make sure we are taken care of. The house and the car are not the goals, but if we receive them while staying faithful to God, we need not be ashamed. We must continue to focus on heaven and do the good works we know God wants us to do, His calling for us. We cannot out give God, *Lk 6:38, "Give, and it shall be given unto you; good measure, pressed down, and shaken together, and running over, shall men give into your bosom. For with the same measure that ye mete withal it shall be measured to you again."* The devil wants us to fear the future, so that we will not follow God's calling. This is one of the ways the devil keeps us from shining our light, he wants us to hide and hoard our blessings, so that others will not see the light God has given us. But, God calls us to shine the light He has given us, *Matt 5:16, "Let your light so shine before men, that they may see your good works, and glorify your Father which is in heaven."*

His message is simple, love everyone the way He loves us. This is how his light will be seen and how it will draw others to Him. Each of us has a different calling, a different way of shining our light. It is up to each of us to find our calling. *Heb 2:4, "God also bearing them witness, both with signs and wonders, and with divers miracles, and gifts of the Holy Ghost, according to his own will?"* We ought not waste the gifts He has given us.

God has told us how this story ends and we will explore that in our final chapter!

How does it all end?

Revelation completes the picture of the events that are to occur after the Second Coming of Jesus, which will lead to the end of time. Here they are in chronological order with the minimum amount of commentary:

Satan is imprisoned:

Rev 14:15, "And another angel came out of the temple, crying with a loud voice to him that sat on the cloud, Thrust in thy sickle, and reap: for the time is come for thee to reap; for the harvest of the earth is ripe." God's church is ready and it is time for Jesus to return and collect His eternal family.

Rev 18:2-4, "And he cried mightily with a strong voice, saying, Babylon the great is fallen, is fallen, and is become the habitation of devils, and the hold of every foul spirit, and a cage of every unclean and hateful bird. For all nations have drunk of the wine of the wrath of her fornication, and the kings of the earth have committed fornication with her, and the merchants of the earth are waxed rich through the abundance of her delicacies. And I heard another voice from heaven, saying, Come out of her, my people, that ye be not partakers of her sins, and that ye receive not of her plagues."

1 Thes 4:16-17, "For the Lord himself shall descend from heaven with a shout, with the voice of the archangel, and with the trump of God: and the dead in Christ shall rise first: Then we which are alive and remain shall be caught up together with them in the clouds, to meet the Lord in the air: and so shall we ever be with the Lord."

Rev 20:1-3, "And I saw an angel come down from heaven, having the key of the bottomless pit and a great chain in his hand. And he laid hold on the dragon, that old serpent, which is the Devil, and Satan, and bound him a thousand years, And cast him into the bottomless pit, and shut him up, and set a seal upon him, that he should deceive the nations no more, till the thousand years should be fulfilled: and after that he must be loosed a little season."

We will reign with Jesus for One Thousand Years:

Rev 7:12-17, "Saying, Amen: Blessing, and glory, and wisdom, and thanksgiving, and honour, and power, and might, be unto our God for ever and ever. Amen. And one of the elders answered, saying unto me, What are these which are arrayed in white robes? and whence came they? And I said unto him, Sir, thou knowest. And he said to me, These are they which came out of great tribulation, and have washed their robes, and made them white in the blood of the Lamb. Therefore are they before the throne of God, and serve him day and night in his temple: and he that sitteth on the throne shall dwell among them. They shall hunger no more, neither thirst any more; neither shall the sun light on them, nor any heat. For the Lamb which is in the midst of the throne shall feed them, and shall lead them unto living fountains of waters: and God shall wipe away all tears from their eyes."

Rev 20:5, "But the rest of the dead lived not again until the thousand years were finished. This is the first resurrection." Those who have died without accepting Jesus' offer will remain dead for the thousand years of peace and rest on the earth.

Satan is released and he deceives the rest of the world and they go to fight the saints:

Rev 20:7-9, "And when the thousand years are expired, Satan shall be loosed out of his prison, And shall go out to deceive the nations which are in the four quarters of the earth, Gog, and Magog, to gather them together to battle: the number of whom is as the sand of the sea. And they went up on the breadth of the earth, and compassed the camp of the saints about, and the beloved city: and fire came down from God out of heaven, and devoured them."

Remember, the judgment that decides the names to be found in the book of life was started in 1844, now we see everyone that is not found in the book of life is subject to sentencing and will be thrown into the lake of fire where Satan, the beast and the false prophet are:

Rev 20:11-15, "And I saw a great white throne, and him that sat on it, from whose face the earth and the heaven fled away; and there was found no place for them. And I saw the dead, small and great, stand before God; and the books were opened: and another book was opened, which is the book of life: and the dead were judged out of those things which were written in the books, according to their works. And the sea gave up the dead which were in it; and death and hell delivered up the dead which were in them: and they were judged every man according to their works. And death and hell were cast into the lake of fire. This is the second death. And whosoever was not found written in the book of life was cast into the lake of fire."

This does not mean they will be alive and feeling this torment. It means that for all eternity, the devil, his followers and death will no longer be in the presence of God. They will have burned to ash in the lake of fire, *Ps 37:20*, *"But the wicked shall perish, and the enemies of the Lord shall be as the fat of lambs: they shall consume; into smoke shall they consume away."* and *Matt 13:40*, *"As therefore the tares are gathered and burned in the fire; so shall it be in the end of this world."* Everything in the lake of fire, the beast, the false prophet, Satan and death will be consumed. They will perish, *Jn 3:16*, *"For God so loved the world, that he gave his only begotten Son, that whosoever believeth in him should not perish, but have everlasting life."* Only those who have accepted Jesus will have everlasting life! This marks the end of time. Everything that follows will be part of eternity.

Then a new heaven and a new earth are created:

Rev 21:1, "And I saw a new heaven and a new earth: for the first heaven and the first earth were passed away; and there was no more sea."

A New Jerusalem descends from heaven and God will dwell with the His family for eternity:

Rev 21:2-4, "And I John saw the holy city, new Jerusalem, coming down from God out of heaven, prepared as a bride adorned for her husband. And I heard a great voice out of heaven saying, Behold, the tabernacle of God is with men, and he will dwell with them, and they shall be his people, and God himself shall be with them, and be their God. And God shall wipe away all tears from their eyes; and there shall be no more death, neither sorrow, nor crying, neither shall there be any more pain: for the former things are passed away."

Rev 21:6, "And he said unto me, It is done. I am Alpha and Omega, the beginning and the end. I will give unto him that is athirst of the fountain of the water of life freely."

Heaven, what is it and what will it be like?

Before my father-in-law died he used to ponder the question of heaven. He hated the thought that we might just sit around all day on clouds playing harps. Hopefully, we have a lot more to look forward to than that.

God will create a new Heaven and a new earth, which will be the eternal home of the family He is creating. *Rev 21:1, "And I saw a new heaven and a new earth: for the first heaven and the first earth were passed away; and there was no more sea."*

What will this New Jerusalem be like? *Rev 21:10-23, "And he carried me away in the spirit to a great and high mountain, and shewed me that great city, the holy Jerusalem, descending out of heaven from God, Having the glory of God: and her light was like unto a stone most precious, even like a jasper stone, clear as crystal; And had a wall great and high, and had twelve gates, and at the gates twelve angels, and names written thereon, which are the names of the twelve tribes of the children of Israel: On the east three gates; on the north three gates; on the south three gates; and on the west three gates. And the wall of the city had twelve foundations, and in them the names of the twelve apostles of the Lamb. And he that talked with me had a golden reed to measure the city, and the gates thereof, and the wall thereof. And the city lieth foursquare, and the length is as large as the breadth: and he measured the city with the reed, twelve thousand furlongs. The length and the breadth and the height of it are equal. And he measured the wall thereof, an hundred and forty and four cubits, according to the measure of a man, that is, of the angel. And the building of the wall of it was of jasper: and the city was pure gold, like unto clear glass. And the foundations of the wall of the city were garnished with all manner of precious stones. The first foundation was jasper; the second, sapphire; the third, a chalcedony; the fourth, an emerald; The fifth, sardonyx; the sixth, sardius; the seventh, chrysolyte; the eighth, beryl; the ninth, a topaz; the tenth, a chrysoprasus; the eleventh, a jacinth; the twelfth, an amethyst. And the twelve gates were twelve pearls: every several gate was of one pearl: and the street of the city was pure gold, as it were transparent glass. And I saw no temple therein: for the Lord God Almighty and the Lamb are the temple of it. And the city had no need of the sun, neither of the moon, to shine in it: for the glory of God did lighten it, and the Lamb is the light thereof."* The New Jerusalem is where we will live for all eternity. A furlong is about one eighth of a mile, so our city will be a very large cube, fifteen hundred miles wide, long and tall? Fifteen hundred miles, can you visualize the size of this city, big enough to cover half of America! This is where we will live and the heavens will be our playground.

What will our heavenly playground look like? *Gen 2:8, "And the Lord God planted a garden eastward in Eden; and there he put the man whom he had formed. And out of the ground made the Lord God to grow every tree that is pleasant to the sight, and good for food; the tree of life also in the midst of the garden, and the tree of knowledge of good and evil. And a river went out of Eden to water the garden; and from thence it was parted, and became into four heads."* and *Ps 19:1, "The heavens declare the glory of God; the skies proclaim the work of his hands."* We can look today at our world and the skies above to get an answer to this question. *Is 41:18, "I will open rivers in high places, and fountains in the midst of the valleys: I will make the wilderness a pool of water, and the dry land springs of water. I will plant in the wilderness the cedar, the shittah tree, and the myrtle, and the oil tree; I will set in the desert the fir tree, and the pine, and the box tree together: That they may see, and know, and consider, and understand together, that the hand of the Lord hath done this, and the Holy One of Israel hath created it."* We will have gardens, waterfalls, ponds, and crystals, green grass and beautiful flowers of all colors, all kinds of animals, etc. Our world has over 250,000 species of flowering plants alone; can we imagine what God will do with Heaven? God will make Heaven infinitely more beautiful than this world. Everything in Heaven will bring us pleasure. It will be perfect. The Hubble telescope has pictures of what the skies really look like, once we get away from our atmosphere. This link takes you the Hubble picture gallery so that you can view beauty God has already created: <u>Hubble Picture Gallery.</u>[73] In short, we will be surrounded by beauty beyond our imagination!

Who will be there? Everyone who embraced the light they where given while they were on earth. Everyone who chooses to do the will of the Father, whether they knew they were embracing it, or not. *Matt 12:50, "For whosoever shall do the will of my Father which is in heaven, the same is my brother, and sister, and mother."* Since, we know there will be people from every nation, this world will be well represented in the next, *Acts 10:34-35, "Then Peter opened his mouth, and said, Of a truth I perceive that God is no respecter of persons: But in every nation he that feareth him, and worketh righteousness, is accepted with him."* and *Rev 14:6, "And I saw another angel fly in the midst of heaven, having the everlasting gospel to preach unto them that dwell on the earth, and to every nation, and kindred, and tongue, and people,"* People from every race, people of every color and people who one time believed in every other religion on earth, will be in Heaven.

Who will not be there? Those who refuse to do the will of God will not be in heaven, *Matt 7:21, "Not every one that saith unto me, Lord, Lord, shall enter into the kingdom of heaven; but he that doeth the will of my Father which is in heaven."* Being religious will not get us into Heaven. *Rev 21:4, "And God shall wipe away all tears from their eyes; and there shall be no more death, neither sorrow, nor crying, neither shall there be any more pain: for the former things are passed away."* There will be no poor, no sick, no tears, no fear, no pain, and no disheartened people in Heaven. There will be nothing to fear and every desire will be fulfilled in heaven. This is possible, because only those who accept God's invitation will be there.

Will we be married? Not the way we think of marriage. We will be able to spend time with anyone there, and hopefully, our earthly spouses will be at the top of our lists. *Mk 12:25, "When the dead rise, they will neither marry nor be given in marriage; they will be like the angels in heaven."* I wonder what the angels are like? What we do know is that we will be one big happy family, *Eph 3:14-15, "For this cause I bow my knees unto the Father of our Lord Jesus Christ, Of whom the whole family in heaven and earth is named,"*

Will we have friends? Everyone there will be our friend, they will love us and we will love them, each will have the desire to serve everyone else, *Lk 15:7, "I tell you that in the same way there will be more rejoicing in heaven over one sinner who repents than over ninety-nine righteous persons who do not need to repent."* This means there will be plenty of partying in Heaven, since we will all be saved sinners. *Matt 5:44-45 – "But I say unto you, Love your enemies, bless them that curse you, do good to them that hate you, and pray for them which despitefully use you, and persecute you; That ye may be the children of your Father which is in heaven: for He maketh his sun to rise on the evil and on the good, and sendeth rain on the just and on the unjust."* If this is how He wants us to treat our enemies on earth, imagine how great it will be there, where everyone will be our friend?

What will we do? There is no limit to what we will do. *Matt 6:10, "Thy kingdom come, Thy will be done in earth, as it is in heaven."* We will be doing the very same things in Heaven that we are now doing on earth, with one limitation, there will be no evil. *Ex 33:11, "And the Lord spake unto Moses face to face, as a man speaketh unto his friend."* He wants to talk with us as friends and when we are in Heaven we will talk with all of our friends, God, our old friends and our many new ones. Considering there will be billions of them, this could take some time, but then we do have all of eternity. *Is 1:18, "Come now, and let us reason together, saith the Lord..."* We will be able to sit and reason with God any time we want and get answers to all of our questions, like why did my grandmother suffer the last few years of her life? Or, why did God make so many stars

251

when we can only see a small number of them? *2 Chron 34:12, "...all that could skill of instruments of musick."* God has given each of us unique gifts, skills, and talents. When we are in Heaven we will use them to amuse ourselves, and others. I cannot wait to see Doctor J flying through the air, again, making a one-handed flip shot! We will play and laugh every day. We can finally read those books we have wanted to read. We will have the privilege of worshiping every Sabbath with God. *Ps 115:3, "But our God is in the heavens: he hath done whatsoever he hath pleased."* We will do whatever we please!

Where will we live? We will all live in mansions, in the New Jerusalem that John so beautifully described in Revelation 21 above and as Paul told us in, *2 Cor 5:2, "Meanwhile we groan, longing to be clothed instead with our heavenly dwelling,"* and John in, *Jn 14:2, "In my Father's house are many mansions: if it were not so, I would have told you. I go to prepare a place for you."*

What will we eat and drink? Whatever we want! *Gen 2:16, "And the Lord God commanded the man, saying, Of every tree of the garden thou mayest freely eat: But of the tree of the knowledge of good and evil, thou shalt not eat of it: for in the day that thou eatest thereof thou shalt surely die."* Since, we can no longer die and the evil issue will have been dealt with, we will be able to eat any fruit in the garden! *Gen 3:18, "Thorns also and thistles shall it bring forth to thee; and thou shalt eat the herb of the field;"* We will surely still be able to eat anything from the field. *Gen 18:7, "And Abraham ran unto the herd, and fetcht a calf tender and good, and gave it unto a young man; and he hasted to dress it."* Abraham prepared a calf for the Lord to eat with him. We might have some meat in Heaven. *Gen 21:19, "And God opened her eyes, and she saw a well of water; and she went, and filled the bottle with water, and gave the lad drink."* I am betting the water in Heaven will be the best tasting water! *Ex 3:8, "And I am come down to deliver them out of the hand of the Egyptians, and to bring them up out of that land unto a good land and a large, unto a land flowing with milk and honey..."* And, of course, there will be milk and honey! *Deut 14:26, "And thou shalt bestow that money for whatsoever thy soul lusteth after, for oxen, or for sheep, or for wine, or for strong drink, or for whatsoever thy soul desireth: and thou shalt eat there before the Lord thy God, and thou shalt rejoice, thou, and thine household,"* It appears that God wants us to enjoy what we eat and drink, my guess is that the wine and strong drink in Heaven will be a little different. I am expecting them to taste great and provide us the feeling of joy without the loss of our decision processes. Well, maybe we cannot know everything about Heaven...until we get there.

Will we sleep? Probably not, we will have been resurrected to our new incorruptible bodies, *1 Cor 15:52, 54, "In a moment, in the twinkling of an eye, at the last trump: for the trumpet shall sound, and the dead shall be raised incorruptible, and we shall be changed. So when this corruptible shall have put on incorruption, and this mortal shall have put on immortality, then shall be brought to pass the saying that is written, Death is swallowed up in victory."* Whether we sleep or not is not that important. However, the fact that our unique part of God's Spirit will be put back into perfect versions of our original bodies, bodies fashioned after Jesus' body, and that we will be living souls who will never die, is important, *Phil 3:20-21, "For our conversation is in heaven; from whence also we look for the Saviour, the Lord Jesus Christ: Who shall change our vile body, that it may be fashioned like unto his glorious body, according to the working whereby he is able even to subdue all things unto himself."* When we are in heaven, we will actually be the people God created us capable of becoming. I do not know about you, but that is a very exciting thought!!!

Heaven, the place I want to spend eternity!

Thank you for taking the journey through the Bible with me! Twenty-seven years ago I decided to read the Bible, in one year. I began by calculating how many pages I would need to read each day and started reading daily. At the end of the year I felt I had a good overview of the content of the Bible, however, I realized that many of the verses I read near the end of the book offered new incite on verses I had read earlier. *Is 28:10, "For precept must be upon precept, precept upon precept; line upon line, line upon line; here a little, and there a little:"* So, for the next four years I read the entire Bible each year, over and over, again. Hopefully, our journey together will inspire you to read the entire Bible this coming year. Depending on the Bible you choose to read, you should be able to read five or six pages a day and complete it in one year. The year is going to pass whether you choose to read the Bible, or not. But, I promise you one thing, if you read those five or six pages a day, you will see this world differently. Some of the people you have admired will no longer be admired and many new ones will be admired. Reading the Bible will change many things in your life, as an example, I now only listen to the K-Love radio station. Uplifting Christian music without commercials. No negative messages affecting the way I feel, only inspirational songs and stories that help me better understand God.

Since, we live in a world influenced by the devil, most things are judged by their outward appearances. Look around at the beautiful people we admire. This is not God's way. *1 Sam 16:7, "But the Lord said unto Samuel, Look not on his countenance, or on the height of his stature; because I have refused him: for the Lord seeth not as man seeth; for man looketh on the outward appearance, but the Lord looketh on the heart."* God sees the real person, who we are on the inside, *Ps 44:21, "Shall not God search this out? for he knoweth the secrets of the heart."* Outward appearance can attract us, but only genuine inside beauty keeps us forever. The devil wants us to think we can get the same satisfaction from outward appearance. It is an illusion. True, eternal satisfaction comes only from love. Only love, which is an internal beauty, can keep us satisfied. Our world lives in the confusion and strife the devil propagates. This confusion and strife has us running to the first thing we see that offers us hope of satisfaction, which usually is driven by its outward illusion alone. We run to the beautiful woman, fancy car, expensive house, and positions of power, only to find that ultimately they do not satisfy us unless they are accompanied by love. Those who are not beautiful on the inside are like a drug; each time we go to them we need a little more, to reach the same high. There is no end to this cycle, except the death that waits at the end of the last high.

Only God and His Word offer us the true happiness we unknowingly seek. *Ps 37:4, "Delight thyself also in the Lord: and he shall give thee the desires of thine heart."* Until we realize that the Old Testament and the New Testament fit together like a hand and a glove, we will not be able to properly interpret the Truth of the Bible. Context is important, not only the context of each individual chapter or book, but even more importantly, how each one fits into the context of the entire Bible. Words have multiple meanings and verses can have multiple messages imbedded within them. This is the secret of the Bible, this is what makes it so unique, and this is what shows us it is the inspired Word of God. It is very complex and at the same time very simple. There are multiple themes running through the Bible, but the most important one is love. God is pure love and He tells us this in numerous ways from the creation to the second coming of Jesus. *1 Jn 4:8, "He that loveth not knoweth not God; for God is love."* It is up to each of us to study the Bible until we see the individual message God has in it for each of us. We might think that it is impossible to write individual messages to billions of people and embed them within one book. God is in the impossible business, *Mk 10:27, "And Jesus looking upon them saith, With men it is impossible, but not with God: for with God all things are possible."* Some people only need to hear one verse to accept Jesus as their savior. Most of us think we are too intelligent to believe this simple message, or maybe we are just too selfish. I certainly fell into the too selfish category.

We think, "Why would an amazing being like God give us such a simple message?" or "Why would such a powerful being as God care about me?" The truth is, He loves each of us equally, and He knows that we each need to hear the message in different ways to understand the depth of His love. *Jn 3:16, "For God so loved the world, that he gave his only begotten Son, that whosoever believeth in him should not perish, but have everlasting life."* He is not giving us many different messages; it is the same message, presented many different ways. His message is not meant for just the John's or Paul's or Peter's of this world, He gave up His life so that whosoever chooses to believe will have eternal life. Because He loves all of us, God created a Bible that includes individual messages to each of us. If only we would take the time to read it, with the desire to find our individual message, we would understand it is true! Only five or six pages a day!

God calls all of us to read the Bible. *Is 1:18, "Come now, and let us reason together, saith the Lord: though your sins be as scarlet, they shall be as white as snow; though they be red like crimson, they shall be as wool."* He wants each of us to learn to interpret the message He has sent us. For more on the basic hermeneutical principles, check out this link: Hermeneutic Principles.[74]

By the grace of God I have had my conversation in this world and I thank you for your part in it, *2 Cor 1:12, "For our rejoicing is this, the testimony of our conscience, that in simplicity and godly sincerity, not with fleshly wisdom, but by the grace of God, we have had our conversation in the world, and more abundantly to you-ward."*

There currently are many study books/guides created to help people in their study of the Bible. Each one of these books/guides reaches a unique group of people. Apparently, there are some people out there who do not know they love God. This is because they do not know God loves them, 1 Jn 4:19, *"We love him, because he first loved us."* With God's blessing this book will help some people connect with God's Word.

Appendix A

URL's for Links provided

[1] Hubblesite Of Images. URL: http://hubblesite.org/images/gallery
[2] Planet Earth Plan Or Accident? URL: http://www.icr.org/article/planet-earth-plan-or-accident/
[3] How The Eye Works. URL: http://www.webexhibits.org/causesofcolor/1G.html
[4] What The Adventists Get Right. URL: https://www.huffingtonpost.com/2014/07/31/seventh-day-adventists-life-expectancy_n_5638098.html
[5] Fastest Growing Church In US. URL: http://usatoday30.usatoday.com/news/religion/2011-03-18-Adventists_17_ST_N.htm
[6] Jesus' Fulfilling Of Bible Prophecy. URL: http://www1.cbn.com/biblestudy/biblical-prophecies-fulfilled-by-jesus
[7] Info On The Dead Sea Scrolls. URL: http://www.deadseascrolls.org.il/?locale=en_US
[8] Biblical Jericho Archaeological Evidence. URL: http://www.biblearchaeology.org/post/2008/05/Did-the-Israelites-Conquer-Jericho-A-New-Look-at-the-Archaeological-Evidence.aspx
[9] Bible Prophecy Fulfilled. URL: http://www.creationstudies.org/articles/who-is-god/332-biblical-prophecies
[10] The 12 Steps. URL: http://www.hazeldenbettyford.org/articles/twelve-steps-of-alcoholics-anonymous
[11] http://www.ltw.org URL: http://www.ltw.org
[12] Lk 15:11-32 URL: https://www.biblegateway.com/passage/?search=lk15%3A11-32&version=KJV
[13] Matt 13:18-30. URL: https://www.biblegateway.com/passage/?search=mat13%3A18-30&version=KJV
[14] Has Bible Prophecy Proven Reliable. URL: http://www.reasons.org/explore/blogs/todays-new-reason-to-believe/read/tnrtb/2003/08/22/fulfilled-prophecy-evidence-for-the-

reliability-of-the-bible

[15] The God Of The Bible Created Everything We See URL: http://www.reasons.org/explore/publications/rtb-101/read/rtb-101/2005/04/01/creation-ex-nihilo

[16] Ken Ham On Six Days Of Creation. URL: https://www.bing.com/videos/search?q=ken+ham+video+on+creation&view=detail&mid=05589C2A2E732571B1D405589C2A2E732571B1D4&FORM=VIRE

[17] The Seven Day Human Rhythm. URL: http://www.livingtheway.org/SabbathArticles/7daycycle.html

[18] Discussion On Decay Rates. URL: https://answersingenesis.org/age-of-the-earth/

[19] Proof Bible Will Never Be Destroyed. URL: http://truthmagazine.com/archives/volume19/TM019211.html

[20] Prophecy Of Israel Becoming A Nation. URL: http://www.1260-1290-days-bible-prophecy.org/bible_prophecy-Israel-nation-1260-years-x2-A-1.htm

[21] Life Mapping With Jesus Book. URL: https://issuu.com/friendofgod

[22] Putting God First. URL: http://brandonweb.com/sermons/sermonpages/matthew18.htm

[23] Worshipping Idols. URL: https://www.gotquestions.org/idol-worship.html

[24] Honoring Our Parents. URL: https://www.gotquestions.org/honor-father-mother.html

[25] Caring For Aging Parents. URL: https://bible.org/seriespage/18-between-child-and-parent-honoring-father-and-mother-exodus-2012

[26] Christian Martyrs. URL: http://www.foxnews.com/world/2013/06/02/vatican-spokesman-claims-100000-christians-killed-annually-because-faith.html

[27] Discussion on racism. URL: https://childline.org.uk/info-advice/bullying-abuse-safety/crime-law/racism-racial-bullying/

[28] Atheists Views On Stealing. URL: http://www.quora.com/why-is-stealing-wrong-1

[29] The Consequences Of Lying. URL: http://tipsforsuccessblog.blogspot.com/2009/06/tipsforsuccess-consequences-of-lying.html

[30] Lack Of Trust Leading To Killing. URL: http://www.foxnews.com/world/2016/06/06/isis-kills-dozens-its-own-in-hunt-for-spies.html?intcmp=hpbt1

[31] Suicide In The US. URL: https://en.wikipedia.org/wiki/Suicide_in_the_United_States

[32] Biblical Advice On Diet URL: http://www.biblestudy.org/basicart/the-

bible-diet.html

[33] Biblical Foods By Verse. URL: http://christianity.about.com/od/biblefactsandlists/qt/foodsofthebible.htm

[34] Circaseptan Rhythm In Humans. URL: http://www.livingtheway.org/SabbathArticles/7daycycle.html

[35] Circadian Rhythm In Humans. URL: https://en.wikipedia.org/wiki/Circadian_rhythm

[36] The 57 Prophets God Sent. URL: http://www.jewfaq.org/prophet.htm

[37] The Land God Promised The Jewish People. URL: http://www.differentspirit.org/articles/boundaries.php

[38] The Story Of Six Day War. URL: https://www.britannica.com/event/Six-Day-War

[39] Good and Evil. URL: https://issuu.com/friendofgod

[40] Hitler's death. URL: https://en.wikipedia.org/wiki/Death_of_Adolf_Hitler

[41] Saddam's capture. URL: https://en.wikipedia.org/wiki/Operation_Red_Dawn

[42] Bible Translators Killed URL: http://www.foxnews.com/world/2016/04/03/bible-charity-vows-to-continue-translation-work-after-murders-four-employees.html?intcmp=hpbt3

[43] Water Tower With Church Name URL: http://www.poncapost.com/local/church-name-broken-arrow-water-tower-draws-threats-lawsuits

[44] Christians Targeted For Extermination URL: http://www.wsj.com/articles/aiding-the-christians-targeted-by-isis-for-extermination-1449876127

[45] Christians Targeted By Oregon Shooter URL: http://www.chron.com/crime/article/Christians-targeted-executed-by-Oregon-shooter-6545261.php

[46] Easter Bombing URL: http://www.foxnews.com/world/2016/03/28/at-least-70-killed-in-pakistan-bombing-targeting-christians.html

[47] What Is Existentialism? URL: https://www.youtube.com/watch?v=YaDvRdLMkHs

[48] History Of The Waldensians. URL: http://www.christian-history.org/waldensians.html

[49] Antiquities Of The Jews. URL: https://en.wikipedia.org/wiki/Antiquities_of_the_Jews

[50] Josephus On Jesus. URL: https://en.wikipedia.org/wiki/Josephus_on_Jesus

[51] The Annals URL: https://en.wikipedia.org/wiki/Annals_(Tacitus)
[52] Nero's Persecution Of The Christians URL: https://en.wikipedia.org/wiki/Tacitus_on_Christ
[53] The Annuals, Book 14 Chapter 44. URL: https://en.wikisource.org/wiki/The_Annals_(Tacitus)/Book_15#44
[54] Pliny The Younger URL: https://en.wikipedia.org/wiki/Pliny_the_Younger
[55] Pliny The Younger On Christians. URL: https://en.wikipedia.org/wiki/Pliny_the_Younger_on_Christians
[56] Sextus Julius Africanus URL: https://en.wikipedia.org/wiki/Sextus_Julius_Africanus
[57] Thallus URL: https://en.wikipedia.org/wiki/Thallus_(historian)
[58] Phlegon URL: https://en.wikipedia.org/wiki/Phlegon_of_Tralles
[59] Lucian. URL: https://en.wikipedia.org/wiki/Lucian
[60] The Twelve Caesars. URL: https://en.wikipedia.org/wiki/The_Twelve_Caesars
[61] Prophecies Jesus Fulfilled. URL: https://www.thoughtco.com/prophecies-of-jesus-fulfilled-700159
[62] John Rylands Fragment URL: https://en.wikipedia.org/wiki/Rylands_Library_Papyrus_P52
[63] Chester Beatty Papyrus URL: https://en.wikipedia.org/wiki/Chester_Beatty_Papyri
[64] Bodmer Papyrus URL: https://en.wikipedia.org/wiki/Bodmer_Papyri
[65] Evidence Of Christ's Existence. URL: http://carm.org/manuscript-evidence - footnote1_fd7t7h5
[66] 365 Prophecies Jesus Fulfilled. URL: http://bibleprobe.com/365messianicprophecies.htm
[67] chapter 13 of Isiah URL: https://www.biblegateway.com/passage/?search=is13&version=KJV
[68] Roman Catholic Persecution Of Reformers. URL: https://en.wikipedia.org/wiki/Reformation
[69] Jesuits Re-interpret Scripture. URL: http://www.christiandoctrine.com/christian-doctrine/the-bible/1202-jesuits-others-and-new-bible-versions
[70] Calculation Of The 1,260 Years of Daniel. URL: http://www.bibleprobe.com/archive/messages/314.html
[71] Ezra 7. URL: https://www.biblegateway.com/passage/?search=Ezra7&version=KJV
[72] Discussion Of The Year 1844 AD URL: https://www.amazingfacts.org/media-library/study-guide/e/4995/t/right-on-time-prophetic-appointments-revealed
[73] Hubble Picture Gallery. URL URL:

http://hubblesite.org/images/gallery
[74] Hermeneutic Principles. URL:
https://en.wikipedia.org/wiki/Hermeneutics

Made in the USA
San Bernardino, CA
07 October 2018